So Odd a Mixture

of related interest

The Complete Guide to Asperger's Syndrome
Tony Attwood
ISBN 978 1 84310 495 7

Pretending to be Normal
Living with Asperger's Syndrome
Liane Holliday Willey
Foreword by Tony Attwood
ISBN 978 1 85302 749 9

Alone Together
Making an Asperger Marriage Work
Katrin Bentley
Foreword by Tony Attwood
ISBN 978 1 84310 537 4

Freaks, Geeks and Asperger Syndrome
A User Guide to Adolescence
Luke Jackson
Foreword by Tony Attwood
ISBN 978 1 84310 098 0

All Cats Have Asperger Syndrome
Kathy Hoopmann
ISBN 978 1 84310 481 0

Natural Genius
The Gifts of Asperger's Syndrome
Susan Rubinyi
ISBN 978 1 84310 784 2

A Blessing and a Curse
Autism and Me
Caiseal Mór
ISBN 978 1 84310 573 2

The Genesis of Artistic Creativity
Asperger's Syndrome and the Arts
Michael Fitzgerald
ISBN 978 1 84310 334 9

Asperger's Syndrome and High Achievement
Some Very Remarkable People
Ioan James
ISBN 978 1 84310 388 2

So Odd a Mixture

Along the Autistic Spectrum in 'Pride and Prejudice'

Phyllis Ferguson Bottomer

Forewords by Tony Attwood
and Eileen Sutherland

Jessica Kingsley Publishers
London and Philadelphia

First published in 2007
by Jessica Kingsley Publishers
116 Pentonville Road
London N1 9JB, UK
and
400 Market Street, Suite 400
Philadelphia, PA 19106, USA

www.jkp.com

Library of Congress Cataloging in Publication Data
Ferguson Bottomer, Phyllis, 1953-
    So odd a mixture : along the autistic spectrum in Pride and prejudice / Phyllis Fergu-
son Bottomer ; forewords by Eileen Sutherland and Tony Attwood.
        p. cm.
    Includes bibliographical references and index.
    ISBN-13: 978-1-84310-499-5 (pbk. : alk. paper) 1. Austen, Jane, 1775-1817.
Pride and prejudice. 2. Austen, Jane, 1775-1817--Characters. 3. Autism in literature. I.
Title.
    PR4034.P73F47 2007
    823'.7--dc22

                                                            2007016445

British Library Cataloguing in Publication Data
A CIP catalogue record for this book is available from the British Library

ISBN 978 1 84310 499 5

Printed and bound in the United States by Thomson-Shore, Inc.

I dedicate this book with love to my parents,
Ross Goodrich Ferguson and Joan Bunting Ferguson,
and to my parents-in-law,
Alan Robert Bottomer and Jean Stewart Wallace Bottomer

Contents

Foreword

We know that people who have Asperger's syndrome are unusual. Their personalities, interests and abilities mark them out as different. In the twenty-first century, the characteristics are described by clinicians, scientific observers and analyzers of human behaviour, but in past centuries, they were described by another group of astute observers and analyzers – authors. Jane Austen was an astute observer of people and relationships and she describes and obviously knew people who today could have been referred to a clinician for a diagnostic assessment for Asperger's syndrome.

A clinician determines whether someone has the required number of specified characteristics of Asperger's syndrome to warrant a diagnosis, somewhat like completing a 100 piece jigsaw puzzle. Each jigsaw piece is one of the characteristics originally described by the paediatrician Hans Asperger in the late 1930s, or a characteristic identified by subsequent clinical experience and research. We all have some parts of the puzzle, the principle diagnostic question is, are there enough characteristics for a formal diagnosis?

I have read *Pride and Prejudice* for pleasure, thoroughly enjoying the story, humour, dialogue and descriptions. It is one of my favourite novels. But I also read Jane Austen's descriptions of the characters and their conversations as a clinician. I endorse the proposition of Phyllis Ferguson Bottomer in *So Odd a Mixture* that certain key characters in *Pride and Prejudice* have more than their fair share of the characteristics of Asperger's syndrome.

Clearly a clinician would need more information upon which to make a diagnosis than the entertaining and insightful descriptions of Jane Austen. The diagnosis of some of the central characters is conjecture. However, there is considerable value in the proposition. The family dynamics and relationships, thoughts and feelings in Pride and Prejudice are as relevant today as two centuries ago. People still fall in love with someone who has the characteristics of Asperger's syndrome, families still try to adjust to those characteristics and people with Asperger's syndrome still fall in love with someone who is socially insightful, someone at the other end of the continuum of social understanding.

So Odd a Mixture can be read by admirers of the novels of Jane Austen for a new perspective on the characters: by clinicians, to identify the characteristics of Asperger's syndrome as perceived by an astute observer of people and relationships; by those who have Asperger's syndrome, who may be encouraged that they could achieve a life-long relationship; and by the general public, who may appreciate that first impressions may not be accurate when meeting someone with Asperger's syndrome.

Reading *Pride and Prejudice* and *So Odd a Mixture* may give the reader the impression that most of the landed gentry in Britain in the nineteenth century had Asperger's syndrome. The characters described by Jane Austen were probably not a representative sample of the aristocracy and clergy. However, it may explain why the British seem to have a natural understanding and familiarity with the concept of Asperger's syndrome as a description of valued members of British society.

Tony Attwood, author of Asperger's Syndrome
and The Complete Guide to Asperger's Syndrome

Foreword

I have been reading Jane Austen's *Pride and Prejudice* since I was fifteen – a lifetime of delightful reading. I soon went on to the other novels; the more I read them the more I enjoyed them. Like so many other Janeites, I develop a greater appreciation of her books as I learn more about the characters and about Jane Austen herself.

Now Phyllis Ferguson Bottomer has given us a treasure. She has studied the characters in Pride and Prejudice from the point of view of a speech language pathologist. She looks at each character in turn, analyses personality and behaviour, and asks 'Why did he or she do or say that?' Mr Bennet is self-centred, thinking mainly of his own comforts. He neglects his daughters, scorns his wife, and makes no real provision for their future. Mrs Bennet speaks too loudly, and fails to respond to the facial expressions and gestures of others. Another character is silent and awkward at the assembly ball, appearing ill-mannered, ungracious and autocratic.

These attitudes and behaviours can be symptoms of autism, in a mild or extreme form, leading that person to the strange actions we read about. I found the most interesting chapter was 'How did Austen Know?' Phyllis proposes the answer – Austen did it by sheer steady, close observation of her family members, friends, neighbours. There was no medical knowledge or studies of this condition at the time. The people were considered to be odd, strange, dour, or raucous and excitable. Sometimes several members of a family showed these symptoms; some in Jane Austen's own family. She watched and wondered, wrote down what she observed, and made use of it all in her characters. Now medical professionals can understand and appreciate what she described.

Phyllis's teaching experience and interest in language are shown in her writing style – smooth, lucid, flowing easily, no matter how complex the situation she is writing about. I am a compulsive reader of all sorts of books, but never have I read a psychological analysis so easy to understand.

We shall always appreciate these new insights into the personalities and behaviour of the people in the novel, and this reinforcement of our belief in the genius of Austen's characterizations.

Eileen Sutherland,
President of the Jane Austen Society of North America (1988–92)

Acknowledgements

Gratitude needs to stretch back through a lifetime.

My thank yous start with my parents and my three aunts – Mary, Nancy and Brenda Bunting – who ensured that I was raised surrounded by books and occasionally suggested that I should write one of my own some day.

Next I am grateful to my Grade IV and V teacher, Mr Jack Dawes, who gave me the unconditional positive acceptance that helps a child to grow, and who wrote in my autograph book 'You have a great gift in that you can wonder at many things; never lose it.'

My heartfelt thanks must also be expressed to Dr Tony Attwood, whose wise and readable book, *Asperger's Syndrome* (1998), helped me to better understand some of my students, as well as some of the particularly puzzling people I have encountered in my life. His encouraging words about my writing have been greatly appreciated.

This volume would never have existed if a very dear elderly friend, Marg Clarke, had not invited me to come along with her to my first Jane Austen Society of North America (JASNA) meeting on 28 October 2000. Particular gratitude must also be expressed to two other members of our Vancouver branch: Eileen Sutherland, for her affirming comments and Jean Oriente, who, when I first approached her about speaking on this topic, responded with such confidence-building enthusiasm that I was launched on my way. My thanks also to the JASNA branches in Toronto and London, Ontario, and to the JASA branches in Sydney, New South Wales, and Perth, Western Australia, who were curious and courageous enough to take a chance on an unknown speaker offering 'so odd a topic'!

I am grateful also to many others for their invaluable help or interest, including:

- my dear and only sister, Patricia Warsaba, who has been both a confidante and a source of practical advice

- my fellow speech language pathologist, good listener and supportive friend, Bev Lister

- my precious and inspirational friends, Shelley Beardshaw, who so well models her advice that 'You just have to get on with it,' and Liz

Bucknell, who shares, hence understands, the joys and challenges of a cross-Pacific family

- our dear friends who supported my early talks with their interest, practical help and/or attendance, including Bev, Liz, Betty Augaitis, Judy Carpenter, Jane Dawes, Mary Thompson Richards, Kristin McHale, Helen Gotterson, Maura Marshall, Linda Trikarso, and Robert, Bev and Kurt Chapman

- my caring friends, Jan Campito, Ariel Creighton, Karen Koroluk, Gabrielle McLarty, Wendy McNaughton and Debbie Walsh, for their wisdom in so many areas of life

- Dr Selena Lawrie, Dr Chan Gunn, Dawn Siegel and Cathy Russell for their qualities as people and life-improving skills as professionals

- Harriet Jordan for bringing Bernard J. Paris's book to my attention, and Ruth Wilson for publishing advice

- Greg Crowe, James Harris and Hamish Malkin, some of my husband's colleagues, for showing intelligent, positive interest in these ideas despite their bemusement in the early days at my combining talks about Jane Austen with mineral exploration conferences

- my immediate family, as well as my valued colleagues and friends, Rosemary Ramsay and Jill Watson, for reading and commenting on the first draft of this book

- all those who responded to my talks or to my professional assistance with their children by sharing with me some of their personal experiences of adults with possible autistic spectrum disorders; I am deeply honoured by and grateful for their trust

- the many students, parents and staff members of SD #44 North Vancouver with whom I have shared so much of life and from whom I learn daily.

Most especially my thanks must go to my beloved family.

My life is blessed beyond measure with two empathetic and energetic young adult children, Jan and Tim, who have been and are an endless source of pride, joy and love in my life.

I am also blessed by the ongoing love, support and encouragement of my husband and best friend, Lindsay, who has always shown confidence in my ability to tackle and achieve my goals.

Thank you my dearest three.

Introduction

Austen   Autism

Autism   Austen

What can the above words possibly have in common?

Ironically, they are near neighbours in any alphabetical listing. They share four of the same letters. Both are frequently mentioned in the news but usually in quite different sections of the paper or telecast. But these are superficial coincidences – certainly no reason to write a book!

Austen lived from 1775 to 1817; autism was first labelled as such in 1943. The formal recognition of the condition may not have existed in her lifetime but people with it certainly did. Literary descriptions of puzzling characters are among the under-utilized clues that we have for the existence of people with this condition before the middle of the twentieth century. Nowhere are so many so well delineated as in Jane Austen's classic, *Pride and Prejudice*. In this beloved novel she created eight characters on the autistic spectrum while, in her five other major works, another dozen at least make their appearance. Austen did not and could not know what she was describing, but she did so with such precise detail that we can recognize and begin to explain what she could only observe and puzzle over.

I initially read *Pride and Prejudice* in the mid-1960s, while I do not recall hearing the word 'autism' until at university in the early 1970s. The fact that there might be any connection, let alone a strong one, between these two apparently unrelated topics first occurred to me one evening late in 2002 when my husband and I were relaxing watching a video of the 1995 BBC adaptation of the novel. By then I was a speech language pathologist with over 25 years' experience, including extensive involvement in the preceding decade with many students with high-functioning autism or Asperger's syndrome. I had learned so much from these fascinating children and had attended workshops plus immersed myself in textbooks and journal articles to learn more. Suddenly, during the televised drama of *Pride and Prejudice*, a statement by one character on the screen triggered a connection in my mind to something startlingly similar I had recently read in the book *Thinking in Pictures*, by Dr Temple Grandin, a well-regarded animal scientist responsible for the design of one-third of all the livestock-handling facilities in the United States. She is also a woman with autism.

One character fictional, the other one real. Separated by almost 200 years. Yet both people were referring to the rhythm of conversation and their difficulties with it. This challenge and many other of their characteristics made more sense if both were coping with the same fundamental problems.

This idea steeped in my mind for many months until the following summer when I had the opportunity to simultaneously re-read both *Pride and Prejudice* and a modern-day social sciences classic, *Asperger's Syndrome*, by Dr Tony Attwood. As I scribbled reams of notes from my close reading and plastered cross-referencing Post-its in the two books, my awe for the acuity of their powers of observation and for Austen's characterization skills increased by the day. As John Bayley, an essayist on Jane Austen's work has written:

> the pleasures and perceptions Jane Austen offers her reader can be of a very complex kind. Each re-reading strikes us afresh with something newly significant, and some change in the perspective of our own world in relation to hers... Our reaction to her seems intimately, even alarmingly, dependent on our own history. (1968, p.1)

I hope that both your admiration for Miss Austen and your understanding of the often puzzling people with autistic spectrum disorders will also grow as we journey through this beloved novel together using current knowledge about the autistic spectrum as our unique guide.

1

Characters, Caricatures
and Conversations

Jane Austen was not yet 20 years of age when she began *Pride and Prejudice* thus bringing to life the several dozen characters who have enthralled readers ever since. Her telling of a memorable year in the lives of the Bennets and the Darcys, Mr Collins and Mr Wickham, the good Aunt Gardiner and the controlling Aunt Catherine has never been out of print.

Not all of these characters receive equal treatment. Obviously equality of time is impossible as a book needs a central focus, but equality of description is absent as well. Some characters are allowed to become known to us mainly through their own words and actions whereas we are told very clearly how we are to think of others. For example, after the initial chapter of dialogue principally between Mr and Mrs Bennet, any opinions we may have started to form on our own are crisply directed by Austen's labelling their intellectual abilities as being of 'quick parts' for the former and of 'mean understanding' (*Pride and Prejudice*, R. W. Chapman (ed.), third edition, p.5) for the latter. Even for a trait they partially share she selects the more charming word 'caprice' for him while the less flattering 'uncertain temper' (p.5) is used for her. It is similar to our own tendency to describe variations of the same characteristic as 'persistence' in someone we like but as 'stubbornness' in someone we don't.

Bernard J. Paris, in his *Character and Conflict in Jane Austen's Novels: A Psychological Approach*, offers the following opinion about Austen's approach to her characters:

> Jane Austen's authorial personality often strikes me as being perfectionistic. She identifies completely with her perfectionistic characters, empathizes with their plight, and shares many of their traits. Her novels are an affirmation of her own high standards and a criticism of those who do not live up to them. The novels frequently leave the impression that life consists of a few exceptional people, like Austen herself, living in a world which is made up principally of

> knaves and fools... She looks down upon her inferior characters,
> including the simple good ones, with amusement or contempt.
> (1978, p.184)

He comments with admiration on 'her remarkable understanding of a wide range of psychological types' (p.198) and notes that she 'is sympathetic toward the need of sensitive and intelligent people to move away from those who oppress them, and she herself seems to resort to humor to make life tolerable in a world composed largely of fools' (p.197).

In the opinion of D.W. Harding, in his essay 'Character and Caricature in Jane Austen' (1968):

> It seems abundantly clear that in reading Jane Austen's novels we are not intended to take all the figures in the same way. Some are offered as full and natural portraits of imaginable people: others, while certainly referring to *types of people we might easily have come across*, are yet presented with such exaggeration and simplification that our response to them is expected to be rather different. (p.83, my italics)

It appears that Austen, while presenting a full portrait of some of her characters, rather than sketching in the background ones, turns instead to the quite different technique of caricature to capture some of the others.

It is my opinion that many of these apparent caricatures, as well as a few of the more developed characters, seem so exaggerated or unreal because they are Jane Austen's youthful attempts to describe people who are actually on the autistic spectrum. This group, especially at the milder end, contains individuals who are so puzzling, and who possess such seemingly incompatible strengths and weaknesses, that they are extraordinarily challenging to present in a believable way, especially to people who have not met anyone like them. Paris thinks that:

> The great psychological realists have the capacity *to see far more than they can understand*... When they analyze what they have represented or assign their characters illustrative roles, they are *limited by... the conceptual systems of their day.*
>
> The author's understanding of his character is often wrong and almost always oversimple. (1978, p.20, my italics)

[T]hough novelists do, indeed, see more than the rest of us, they are not necessarily wiser or healthier than ordinary [people]. We place too much value, I think, upon their attitudes and beliefs and too little upon their concrete portrayal of reality. (p.21)

Although Jane Austen can see and describe behaviours indicative of the autistic spectrum she cannot understand the underlying issues as those insights had not yet been produced by the psychological/medical/conceptual knowledge of her time. As Paris says in the above quote, her 'attitudes and beliefs' were shaped by her period but her 'concrete portrayal of [the] reality' of human interaction is less affected. The portraits she created of people through their conversation capture the reality of the different abilities that they bring to this seemingly simple task. Tellingly, most of her 'caricatures' can be identified by their poor conversational skills just as can most people on the spectrum. The two groups overlap significantly. Conversation is crucial in reality and in this piece of fiction.

When my then teenaged daughter first read *Pride and Prejudice* she wrote the following in the journal in which she faithfully records both the titles and her impressions of the books that enrich her life:

> Absolutely delightful. I had such a good time reading this book. Dialogue makes up most of the novel which brings home the realization that the art of conversation played a much more significant role in the 1800s than it does in today's society.

Conversation truly is an art, both fine and domestic. Far from being mere idle chatter, it is the lifeblood of a community, with the potential to carry emotional nourishment to each member and to help reduce or remove toxins. There is a reason why we refer to those initial exchanges, particularly with a new acquaintance, as 'social pleasantries' because they can indeed make any interaction pleasant rather than stressful. Failing to converse with others weakens the sense of communal life. If we do not share some of our thoughts and feelings, others feel held at a distance so an opportunity to create more of the myriad threads that weave us together is lost. Failure to show interest in others causes them to feel insecure or unimportant – feelings that can lead them to withdraw slightly, which again reduces that all-important sense of connection. Therefore, the higher the individual's status in the community or in the interaction, the more important it is that he or she engages in conversation in order to help others feel at ease and valued.

As individuals wealthy enough neither to be required to earn their own living nor to do the cooking and cleaning necessary for their daily well-being, the characters in *Pride and Prejudice* have far less minute-by-minute structure in their lives than do those of us with day planners, BlackBerries and/or calendars colour-coded to track the commitments of each family member. Leisure among the gentry in Georgian England was something to be filled not something they had to scramble to find. To occupy this leisure, without our extraordinary variety of technological forms of entertainment, the people of Austen's time, and, indeed, of every time until the last century, had to rely on their inner resources and on the people present in their immediate, physical community. The ability to converse amiably and appropriately with others was key, whether as the principal form of entertainment or secondary to dining, dancing, playing cards or embroidering.

Although conversation is less often the sole entertainment of an entire evening, it is still crucial in our daily affairs. If anything, the ability to make 'small talk' may be more important because, in our mobile worlds, we are more likely to meet new people frequently. Plus people do still come to visit for meals...or even for months!

Having occasionally experienced dinner or house guests whom I now realize were on the spectrum, I can attest that most of those visits were exhausting and unsatisfying, especially if the ratio was skewed and more than one person with ASD was present. In response to the silent, monosyllabic ones everyone else tended at first to talk more or in a livelier way to try to entice them into conversation. Eventually, their limited responses, both verbally and even facially, extinguished the effort the others were putting forward. In contrast, when the guest with ASD was one who frequently launched into monologues, the eyes of the others glazed over or else developed a twitchiness as they watched for the slightest pause to enable them to return to a back-and-forth exchange between the entire group. Either way conversation was a problem rather than a pleasure.

A modern venue where the ability to converse is still highly valued is the book discussion group. In *The Reading Group Book*, the authors could unknowingly be commenting on the challenges of including someone on the spectrum when they draw on their years as participants to observe that:

> A single person can ruin a book discussion by talking too much or getting too far off the topic – but an individual can also spoil a meeting by remaining utterly silent. *A person who says nothing is like a black hole, sucking in energy from everybody else.* It makes others uncomfortable. (Laskin and Hughes 1995, p.82, my italics)

Equally daunting are members similar to Lady Catherine, whose opinions are expressed so loudly and with such firm finality that diverse opinions are discouraged. Since volunteer book groups 'live and breathe on informality, free-wheeling discussion, quirky digression, and humor' (p.81) the often underestimated skills of conversation are crucial to the pleasure of belonging to the group.

Without our being consciously aware of them, as Grice (1975) first pointed out, there are 'rules of discourse by which neurotypical speakers cooperate in their conversations with one another' (Twachtman-Cullen 2006, p.312). These are:

- quantity – provide only the amount of information that is needed by the listener. Too little means that listeners have to ask so many questions that they feel like they are interrogating you; too much means that people are drowning in excessive detail while the flow of the overall conversation stagnates in a backwater

- quality – truthfulness is important; your listener needs to be able to rely on what you say

- relevance – comments should be connected to the topic under discussion; if the topic is changed there needs to be an obvious bridge between the current and new one, or the speaker should use a phrase such as 'I know this is off-topic but...'

- clarity – conversational contributions need to be clear and understandable; this requires some degree of theory of mind or the ability to judge what prior background information the listener already possesses – for example, when telling a funny story about your uncle and his pet skunk, you could assume more prior knowledge on the part of your sister than you could of a stranger from Kazakhstan or Kalimantan who happened to be sitting beside you on a plane; hence your story would differ in terms of the number and type of details you provided and the informality of your construction.

Of these four, the second is usually a strength for people on the spectrum, but the others are often challenges, to varying degrees.

Jane Austen herself was extraordinarily aware of the subtleties of communication skills as, in reference to yet another of her characters, *Northanger Abbey*'s John Thorpe, who also appears to be on the autistic spectrum, she refers to his 'conversation, or rather talk' (1986, p.66) thus recognizing how much more complex the former is than the latter.

> Most people believe that the ability of people to converse is nearly as easy as breathing; it is a process that occurs spontaneously and intuitively. Individuals with social cognitive disorders teach us that this basic process we call conversation actually consists of skills woven together with subtle precision. (Garcia Winner 2002, p.91)

In *Pride and Prejudice* the brilliantly apt conversations Jane Austen creates between her characters provide us with a phenomenal amount of information, both about them and about autistic spectrum disorders.

Part One

Background

You now have an opportunity to choose your own beginning!

Those of you who selected this book because of your interest in the works of Jane Austen are advised to read the first chapter in this section, to acquire some knowledge about autism (see 'Autistic Spectrum Disorders for Janeites' on p. 23).

Those of you with a strong background in the area of autism may want to read the second section, to be introduced to, or reminded of, the main characters in this famous novel (Please turn to '*Pride and Prejudice* for Autism Specialists' on p.31).

Those of you who didn't actually choose this book but were given it by a niece or asked to obtain it by the organizer of your book discussion group are, of course, free to read either, both or neither of the above at your discretion.

2

Autistic Spectrum
Disorders for Janeites

Autism is one of those words that gradually entered our vocabulary without many of us having acquired a clear definition of its meaning. Then there is the term 'Asperger's syndrome', which has appeared even more recently and is often used synonymously with mild or high-functioning autism. Many people seem to know someone whose cousin's son or colleague's nephew has just received this diagnosis. These are words and terms that have only started to move from specialized lexicons to the mainstream during the last decade or two. The labels are new but the condition, although increasing either in identification or frequency or both, is not.

Throughout this book I will tend to use the term 'autistic spectrum disorder' predominantly. To prevent wordiness this will sometimes be referred to as 'on the spectrum' and also as ASD. Some of the people I quote also use AS as a shorter way of referring to Asperger's syndrome. In addition the term neurotypical, or NT, has been created by those at the high-functioning end of the autistic spectrum to refer to people who are classified as 'normal' in behaviour and neurology.

What is autism?

Autism is a neurological condition or developmental disorder that exists throughout the lifespan. There is no known cause or cure, nor is there a medical test to prove its existence. It is a behavioural diagnosis made through observation of a pattern of distinctive ways of interacting with the world and the other people in it.

The concept of a 'Triad of Impairments' as the core problems of those with autism at the high-functioning end of the spectrum was first developed by Lorna Wing (1981). She felt that there were three groups of impairments that affected:

1. relationships

2. communication

3. understanding/imagination.

These problems impact on 'most of the major qualities needed to form friendships and relationships' (Aston 2003, p.14).

The range or degree of impairment in each area varies widely from individual to individual. Their expression of their autistic traits will also vary depending on their intelligence, their other personality characteristics and the environment in which they were raised (including whether one or both of their parents were also on the spectrum). Sometimes the impairments are very subtle indeed, so startling and unexpected when they occur.

What is meant by a 'spectrum disorder'?

A spectrum disorder is one that exists on a continuum from severely impaired at the lower end to blending into the normal range of human variation at the upper. Naturally, it is more difficult to detect at the milder end. The easiest way to visualize the concept of a spectrum is to picture a long line of colour samples showing the subtle shadings from pure white through the dozens of off-whites to greys of darkening intensities to jet black.

In some lights a number of the colour samples could be described as 'white' but, as anyone redecorating knows, when you put those chips in a harsher light or against certain other colours then the degree to which they differ from pure white is stunning. Similarly, although many people with ASD appear fine in most structured and predictable situations, their subtle problems become glaringly obvious when exposed to the more intense 'light' of a large, complex social occasion or a truly intimate moment when deep awareness of another's emotions is required.

What are some specific areas of difficulty?

1. *Theory of mind*, or awareness that other people have different ideas, emotions and perspectives than one does oneself. 'From the age of

around four years, children understand that other people have thoughts, knowledge, beliefs and desires that will influence their behaviour. People with Asperger's syndrome appear to have some difficulty conceptualizing and appreciating the thoughts and feelings of others' (Attwood 1998, p.112). Others will possess theoretical knowledge but not be able to act upon this quickly and appropriately in real-life situations.

2.   *Central coherence*, or knowing what is meaningful and important to attend to. There is a tendency to see details but not to understand how these are connected.

3.   *Executive function*, or the ability to plan and execute complex tasks. Examples of this can range from short-term tasks such as sorting possessions prior to a move, to the long-range planning involved in making and following through on career choices.

4.   *Cognitive shifting*, or the ability to shift focus as appropriate. There is a tendency for those with ASD to maintain focus intently without monitoring the importance of information on the periphery.

5.   *Language processing*, or the ability to understand language simultaneously with hearing it. Sometimes young children on the autistic spectrum are so unresponsive to spoken language that there are fears that they are hearing-impaired. As they mature, even those with high-functioning autism may take longer to learn idioms or to understand verbal humour.

6.   *Dyspraxia*, or an impairment of motor planning. This may cause some to avoid sports and dancing, or to appear slow due to subtle problems initiating movement or speech.

7.   *Awareness of the unwritten rules of conversation*. There is a tendency for those on the autistic spectrum to be at one extreme or the other – either producing a monologue or sitting silent. There can be particular difficulty with initiating conversation and with recognizing that conversations can take place for the social purpose of *experience sharing* as well as the factual purpose of *information sharing*.

8.   *Interpretation of non-verbal cues from facial expressions and gestures*. Researchers have found that 'there is substantial evidence that

individuals with autism are impaired in processing information from people's faces'. However, it appears that 'the face-processing deficits encountered in ASD are not due to a simple dysfunction of the fusiform area, but to more complex anomalies in the distributed network of brain areas involved in social perception and cognition' (Hadjikhani *et al.* 2004, pp.1141–2).

9.   *Sensory sensitivities.* For a significant proportion of those on the spectrum, one or more of their sensory systems perceive ordinary stimuli as unbearably intense. They may object to the feel of certain textures, be overpowered by the smell of cleansers or experience specific sounds as acutely painful. The babble of noise in a large crowd, or sounds that are high pitched and ongoing may be particularly negative. It is as if the revulsion most of us have experienced to the rare sound of fingernails on a chalkboard bombards them many times in the ordinary course of the day.

Does having one of these difficulties mean someone is autistic?

No. It is extremely important to stress that possession of a single one of these characteristics does not mean that an individual is on the autistic spectrum. It is observation of the pattern of characteristics and behaviours over time that leads to the diagnosis. Nor are the majority of shy people autistic. Many individuals are soft-spoken and hesitant, particularly around strangers, but they are also empathetic, able to share in a conversation, and have no diffi-culty with movement or interpreting facial expressions. Shyness is not synonymous with being on the autistic spectrum.

What is the history of this diagnosis?

In his recent book, *Unstrange Minds*, Roy Richard Grinker, an anthropologist and the father of a daughter with autism, stated that 'the discovery of autism wasn't so much a discovery of new truths as a new way of seeing a group of cognitive and social differences.' He added that:

> Although it's likely that autism has existed among humans for at least hundreds of years, until very recently no one thought to create a distinct category for it because our culture – our social, educa-tional, and medical systems – was not ready for it. (Grinker 2007, p.13)

It was first recognized on two continents almost simultaneously but separately:

- in 1943 by Leo Kanner in Baltimore

- in 1944 by Hans Asperger in Vienna.

Coincidentally both doctors gave the traits they observed the same name: *autism* from the Greek for *self*. Because of the Second World War, Hans Asperger's paper describing more mildly affected children wasn't translated into English until 1991. Debate has continued as to whether the two forms of autism are on a continuum or truly separate, with oral language abilities being one of the key dividing features.

Over the last few years the trend has been to refer to *autistic spectrum disorders*, which include classic autism and Asperger's syndrome as well as some rarer disorders.

How many people are on the autistic spectrum?

According to the National Institutes of Health website (www.nichd.nih.gov/autism), approximately 1 in 166 people is estimated to exhibit behaviours that place them along the autistic spectrum.

Are there adults with ASD who have not been diagnosed?

Yes, there certainly are: 40, 60 or 80 years ago, in their childhoods, such a complex array of characteristics was either not recognized as a syndrome or felt to exist only in extremely severe cases when individuals were non-verbal, rarely interacted with others and required assistance in almost every aspect of their lives.

Who are these people at the mild end of the spectrum?

They are people. People we meet in our neighbourhoods and our places of work and worship, in shops and at school, at weddings and funerals. People whom we have met once casually or whom we have known all our lives. Unique and individual, complex and multi-layered. They are people.

By the time you have lived for over half a century, as I have, you have met an extraordinary number of people. Literally hundreds and thousands. In my case two factors increase the number beyond the norm:

1. Professionally, I have a position that at one time brought me into a different school every day of the week, resulting in interactions with a large and ever-changing mix of students, parents and staff.

2. Personally, the first 36 years of my life were highly mobile as I lived in a total of 12 communities spread across five of Canada's provinces, as well as in three communities in two Australian states; therefore, my classmates, neighbours, community members and co-workers changed frequently, bringing me into contact with a larger number and variety of people than if I had remained in one place.

Besides the several dozen children officially diagnosed with ASD with whom I have worked professionally, I have grown to realize that I have encountered a similar or greater number of adults on the spectrum among those I have met in my varied communities and travels. Few of them have been formally diagnosed; instead, at different times in their lives, they have been considered by others to be, 'odd', 'awkward', 'shy', 'brilliant', 'honest to a fault', 'self-centred', 'dedicated', 'spoiled', 'reserved', 'rude', 'quiet', 'a bit different', 'immature', 'not easily side-tracked', 'reliable', 'selfish', 'hard to get to know', 'uncaring', 'eccentric', 'totally focused on their work', 'unfriendly' or 'absolutely impossible'.

Many of these adults I have met are married, and the majority were or are gainfully employed (some successfully, some shakily). They include:

three ministers and two ministers' spouses (one set married to each other)

four professors (two of maths, one of chemistry and one of history)

a number in engineering, geoscience and information technology

several teachers, nurses, secretaries and truck drivers

a pharmacist and several farmers

several musicians and managers

an occupational therapist

a librarian and a lawyer

a school principal

a house painter

a dentist

and, to my amazement, more than one speech language pathologist!

In their wondrous if often puzzling diversity, they are all people.

Is mild autism really a problem?

Mild autism is not a problem in many situations, especially those that are *static* not *fluid*. Steven Gutstein (2000, pp.34–5) described static social systems as those that are relatively predictable so the participant's role and script is clear. Situations such as being a customer in a bank, consultant on an engineering project, or dentist with a patient are examples of static systems. However, fluid systems are much less predictable, with participants having greater flexibility about the topic and type of conversation that occurs. Interacting with fellow guests at a wedding, chatting with your cousin's new girlfriend, or expressing sympathy to a tragically widowed co-worker are fluid interactions.

As her contribution to the debate as to whether being on the spectrum is merely a difference rather than a disability, Maxine Aston, a counsellor, researcher and author of the book *Aspergers in Love: Couple Relationships and Family Affairs*, writes 'it is a different way of thinking that becomes a disability when interaction with others is required' (2003, p.196).

Even with mild forms of autistic spectrum disorders, the impact on personal relationships can be severe on occasion, as others expect normal social functioning and empathy from a family member or partner in a wide variety of fluid situations.

Of the eight characters in *Pride and Prejudice* who exhibit the characteristics of autism, seven are at the high-functioning or Asperger's end of the spectrum. These characters differ from real life in one fascinating and key way: although the current ratios of male to female are believed to be 4:1 for classic autism and 9:1 for Asperger's (Baron-Cohen 2006), in this novel Jane Austen has created the significantly different ratio of 3:5. This fascinating and unusual preponderance of female characters may indicate something about her personal experience with those on the spectrum in her neighbourhood or, indeed, her own family (see Chapter 13).

3

Pride and Prejudice
for Autism Specialists

Jane Austen, the younger daughter of an English parson, began to write *Pride and Prejudice*, originally entitled *First Impressions*, in 1795 while she was in her twentieth year of life after having initially been rejected, her revised manuscript was ultimately printed in 1813 following the publication of another of her novels, *Sense and Sensibility*.

Although no character is born or dies, little mention is made of political or historical events, and there are no murders, bombings or crashes (physical or financial), the story Austen created has been engrossing enough to have held the attention of readers for close to two centuries. In the BBC survey, 'The Big Read', conducted in 2003, *Pride and Prejudice* ranked second as the respondents' best-loved book. Similarly, when Canadian bookseller Chapters/Indigo recently asked over 100,000 of its customers to nominate their favourite books of all time, *Pride and Prejudice* ranked second after a current best-seller.

The people

Famously, in a letter to one of her many nieces, Jane Austen set down her opinion that, when writing a novel, '3 or 4 Families in a Country Village is the very thing to work on' (Le Faye 1995, p.275). In alphabetical order, the families Austen brought to life in *Pride and Prejudice* are as follows.

The Bennets of Longbourn in Hertfordshire
Mr and Mrs Bennet (née Gardiner) have five young and lively, but unmarried, daughters. Their lack of a son means that, when Mr Bennet dies, their entailed home/estate will be inherited by his deceased cousin's son, Mr Collins (aged 25), the rector in the village of Hunsford in Kent, which adjoins Rosings Park, home of the De Bourghs.

The Bennet daughters, in order of age, are: **Jane** (22), **Elizabeth** (20), **Mary** (?), **Kitty** (?) and **Lydia** (15).

The Bingleys, who lease Netherfield in Hertfordshire

Charles Bingley (22), having inherited a fortune – which his father made in trade – is planning to spend some of it purchasing a country estate. When he first comes to Netherfield, his married sister, **Louisa Hurst**, her husband and his unmarried sister, **Caroline Bingley**, are his house guests, as is his closest friend, Fitzwilliam Darcy.

The Darcys of Pemberley in Derbyshire

Fitzwilliam Darcy (28) is the only son from the marriage of his extremely wealthy father to Lady Anne Fitzwilliam. Both his parents are deceased, leaving Mr Darcy as the principal guardian of his much younger sister, **Georgiana** (16).

The De Bourghs of Rosings Park in Kent

The deceased Sir Lewis De Bourgh is survived by his wife, **Lady Catherine** née Fitzwilliam, and his only child and heir, **Anne**.

The Fitzwilliams of — in —

This noble family is headed by the current Earl, who had at least two sisters, the above-mentioned deceased Lady Anne Darcy and the very much alive Lady Catherine De Bourgh. He also has two sons, the elder of whom will inherit his title and the principal part of his estate, while the younger, **Colonel Fitzwilliam**, is pursuing a military career. The Colonel is close friends with his cousin, Mr Darcy.

The Gardiners, originally of the village of Meryton in Hertfordshire

The previous Mr Gardiner was an attorney in Meryton, where one of his daughters, is now married to the current attorney Mrs. Philips'. His other daughter, Mrs. Bennet, made an upwardly mobile marriage to Mr Bennet, a landowner in nearby Longbourn. His son, **Edward Gardiner** of Gracechurch-street in London, is a prosperous and competent businessman with an admirable wife and four young children.

The Lucases of Lucas Lodge near Meryton in Hertfordshire

After being knighted, **Sir William Lucas**, the former mayor of Meryton, abandoned his business interests and purchased a country estate. He and his wife have a large family of at least five unmarried children, including **Charlotte** (27) and **Maria**. Despite their age difference, Charlotte's closest friend is Elizabeth Bennet.

The Wickhams

The deceased steward of the senior Mr Darcy is survived by one son, **Lieutenant George Wickham**. The 'current' Mr Darcy offered Wickham, his father's godson and his own childhood companion, a 'living' or position as the rector in a Derbyshire village but Wickham rejected that occupation, so is currently of 'nowhere in particular' as he serves in the militia that is camped first near Meryton and then moves to Brighton during the time span of the novel.

In my professional opinion, within five of these families are eight characters with traits that place them along the autistic disorders spectrum.

The time period

The principal events in *Pride and Prejudice* take place in England during a single year from October 1811 to October 1812, followed by a briefly mentioned double wedding in December. This pivotal year falls during a short period known as the Regency, when George, the Prince of Wales, was acting as Regent, or substitute, for his father, King George III, who was prevented by mental illness from serving as the monarch. The broader time period is known as Georgian because there were four kings in a row named George.

Additional background information is offered below for those who would like to know more about this period of English history.

- The peerage, or nobility, consisted of 300 or so families. Beneath them were the group to which Jane Austen belonged and about which she wrote her six major novels: 'a gentry society comprising the families of approximately (in 1803) 540 baronets, 350 knights, 6,000 landed squires and 20,000 gentlemen, amounting in total to about 1.4 per cent of the national population and enjoying 15.7 per cent of the national income' (Keymer 2005, p.390).

- The Anglican Church, or Church of England (from which comes the Episcopalian Church in the United States of America), was the dominant Christian denomination. The monarch of England was, and is, also the head of the Church and known as Defender of the Faith.

- A 'gentleman' is a term somewhat difficult to define in that it was used to refer both to socio-economic status and to a way of behaving. In the physical/financial/family sense, a gentleman was someone of 'birth and breeding', particularly on his father's side, who was either a landowner, engaged at a sufficiently high level in one of the 'learned or liberal' professions of the Church, the law or medicine, or else was an officer in the Army or Navy.

- In Georgian England a gentleman was not expected to engage in trade or any sort of business dealings. Ideally he and his family lived off inherited wealth, which was particularly valued if it came from land ownership as 'to own land was to be identified more physically with the nation than to engage in commerce' (Jones 2005, p.269).

- Many landowners owned 'advowsons', or the right to grant 'livings', which meant they could select who held the position as minister in the local parishes on or near their landholdings. These livings varied in affluence as they came with rights to the income from the glebe (church agricultural land) rented out to various farmers. In Jane Austen's time, 'in about half of the country's 10,500 parishes the church livings were the property of local squires' (Southam 2005, p.368).

- Entailment was 'a practice almost universally employed by landowners since its inception in the late seventeenth century, this series of legal devices allowed a man to settle his estate on a yet unborn descendant, in the reasonable assurance that it would survive any extravagance of its immediate inheritor.' This meant that the current owner 'was a life tenant, not an absolute owner, who could not sell or mortgage land except for the purposes specified in the settlement' (Jones 2005, p.270). Therefore, since Longbourn is entailed, Mr Bennet cannot legally sell some of the land in order to provide an inheritance for his daughters.

- Regarding the fortunes whose figures are discussed by the mammas seeking matrimony for their daughters, due to entailment, 'when landed men are introduced in the novels as possessing or heir to a number of thousands of pounds, this is understood as the yearly income from the estate; they usually did not command the capital' (Jones 2005, p.270).

- A gentleman's daughters, if unmarried, lived at home, where they were expected to be supported first by their father and then their brothers. They became governesses only if forced to for financial reasons. No other respectable occupation was open to them as a way of providing for themselves.

- 'Coming out' meant that a young woman had made the move from childhood. She was therefore included in adult gatherings and considered to be available for marriage.

- Christian names were used much less commonly than they are today. Even married couples called each other 'Mr and Mrs', which is why we do not know the first names of the senior Bennets for example.

- Although letter writing to remain in contact with friends and family was a major part of a lady's daily routine, she could not write to a gentleman unless she was related to or engaged to him.

- During the year in which the action of the novel takes place England was in the midst of the Napoleonic Wars against France, which began in 1799 and would continue until 1815. These wars extended to North America, where they are usually known as the War of 1812.

Although blatantly obvious surface differences of fashion and technology exist between our daily lives and those of the people of Regency England, fundamentally most of our underlying human attributes, concerns and desires remain constant. We might not be able to differentiate between the styles of carriages mentioned in *Pride and Prejudice* but we can recognize most of the different types of people portrayed. To paraphrase one of Elizabeth Bennet's observations about Darcy: 'In essentials, I believe, people are very much what they ever were' (p.234).

Part Two

The Bennet Family

4

Mr Collins

'awkward and solemn... often moving wrong without being aware of it' (p.90)

Mr Collins reveals some of his autistic traits before we even meet him. As she listens to his introductory letter, Elizabeth is immediately aware of some of the unusual characteristics with which he presents. In conversation with her father she comments, 'He must be an oddity, I think... I cannot make him out. – There is something very pompous in his stile... [C]an he be a sensible man, sir?' (p.62). Her father responds, 'No, my dear; I think not' and refers to the 'mixture of servility and self-importance in his letter' (p.62).

Once Mr Collins arrives at Longbourn it is instantly obvious that his letter had been an accurate introduction to his personality. 'He was a tall, heavy looking young man of five and twenty. His air was grave and stately, and his manners were very formal' (p.64). His ponderous compliments quickly antagonize his hostesses. Those about their beauty and likelihood of marriage are 'not much to the taste of some of his hearers' while their mother feels that his 'commendation of every thing' furnishing the hall and dining room leads her to the 'mortifying supposition of his viewing it all as his own future property' (p.65). Once Mr Collins is aware that he has insulted them by assuming that one of the daughters cooked the meal he swings too far the other way in his attempt to make amends as he 'continued to apologize for about a quarter of an hour' (p.65).

Mr Collins holds forth at length about the even more heavy-handed compliments that he prepares in advance to offer to his patroness, Lady Catherine De Bourgh, about her daughter. This exemplifies what Frith and Happe have noted: that many autistic people's 'approach to social tasks has been said to resemble slow conscious calculation' (1999, p.7). Mr Collins is completely unaware of the sarcasm in his host's choice of words as Mr Bennet comments that he possesses 'the talent of flattering with delicacy' (p.68). Instead he fulfils Mr Bennet's expectation that he prove to be a source of entertainment by detailing exactly how unspontaneous and wooden his compliments really are. He reveals 'although I sometimes amuse myself with suggesting and arranging such little elegant compliments as may be adapted to ordinary occasions, I always wish to give them as unstudied an air as possible' (p.68).

In his essay, 'The idiolects of the idiots', Jeffrey Herrle refers to how Mr Collins's inability to realize that he is being ridiculed is 'a striking instance of...obliviousness' (2002, p.242). Obliviousness, and many other words that Herrle uses about Mr Collins, are ones that have frequently been applied to people on the spectrum. He includes phrases such as 'obscene self-centredness', 'graceless social skills', 'penchant for excessive language', 'can never truly converse', 'great difficulty listening', 'floridly long-winded and solemnly formal' and 'seems to miss the point' (pp.238–51).

Like Jane Austen herself, Herrle makes very relevant observations about Mr Collins's behaviours, but lacks the understanding that these can also be characteristics associated with autism. Herrle feels that 'it is Mr Collins's vanity [that]...prevents him from ever having a real conversation' (p.251), but the cause lies deeper than that, in the actual physiology of his brain.

Throughout the first evening at Longbourn Mr Collins is 'not inclined to be silent' (p.64). Even Mr Bennet has soon heard enough for his amuse-ment so invites him to read aloud to the ladies. 'After some deliberation he chose Fordyce's Sermons' (p.68) without noticing the no doubt audible gasp produced by the youngest, Lydia. His awareness of how to ingratiate him-self with these prospective brides is strangely limited for a young man on a matrimonial mission. 'Before he had, with very monotonous solemnity, read three pages [Lydia interrupts him]...Mr Collins, much offended, laid aside his book, and said, "I have often observed how little young ladies are inter-ested in books of a serious stamp..."'(p.69). If he knew this, why then did he forge ahead with Fordyce? Like many others on the autistic spectrum, Mr Collins has problems with *central coherence*, or knowing what is meaningful and important to attend to. As Attwood and other researchers have observed, people on the autistic spectrum 'may have knowledge about other people's minds, but they are unable to apply this knowledge effectively' (1998, p.114).

Before selecting the volume of sermons, Mr Collins has rejected the choice offered by his cousins as he 'protested that he never read novels' (p.69). That may merely have been indicative of the opinions of his period and his profession. However, among people on the autistic spectrum, there is a strong preference:

> for reading books for information rather than fictional works, as these portray the characters and personal experience of people and their interactions. Fiction emphasizes social and emotional experiences, in contrast to nonfiction, which does not require an understanding of people and their thoughts, feelings and experiences to the same degree. (Garnett and Attwood 1995, cited in Attwood 1998, p.114)

Similarly, Temple Grandin states firmly that she chooses to read 'factual, nonfictional reading materials' as she has 'little interest in novels with complicated interpersonal relationships' (1992, p.123). Amusingly, Mr Collins would have been particularly bewildered by the novel in which he himself appears!

This incident also shows us that, by criticizing something obviously to the taste of his host family, Mr Collins does not notice that, due to his 'inability to reflect on the difference between [his] own aspirations and those around [him] and to tailor [his] speech accordingly...he has committed the *faux pas* of denouncing [novels] in front of people who obviously enjoy them' (Herrle 2002, p.242). By doing so he exhibits evidence of limited *theory of mind*.

Although Mr Collins's character has already been well sketched for us by his own behaviour, Austen adds details by stating that he 'was not a sensible man, and the deficiency of nature had been but little assisted by education or society; the greatest part of his life having been spent under the guidance of an illiterate and miserly father' (p.70). The 'deficiency of nature' Austen refers to might now be specified as an autistic spectrum disorder. From the reference to his father's stinginess, inability to patch up a quarrel and isolation from society, it is probable that Mr Collins senior also fell somewhere on the spectrum. Austen gives us further information about Mr Collins as she notes that, 'though he belonged to one of the universities, he had merely kept the necessary terms, without forming at it any useful acquaintance' (p.70). At an age and in an environment when people usually make lifelong friendships among their peers he had not been able to maintain such a connection with anyone.

His limited emotional depth is vividly revealed when, having settled on Jane as his first choice for a wife because of 'his strictest notions of what was due to seniority' (p.70), he is informed by Mrs Bennet that that daughter may not be available as she is 'likely to be very soon engaged' (p.71). How quickly he is able to recover from this supposed blow to his heart: 'Mr Collins had only to change from Jane to Elizabeth – and it was soon done – done while Mrs Bennet was stirring the fire' (p.71).

In the next few days the inhabitants of Longbourn and surroundings are provided with endless examples of Mr Collins's inability to converse in a sensible manner. He delivers detailed monologues about places and people unknown to them as he talks to Mr Bennet 'with little cessation, of his house and garden at Hunsford' (p.71) and to his cousins of 'pompous nothings' (p.72). Mr Collins is unable to match his communication style to that of his partners. Sermon-like monologues are somewhat appropriate for congregations but not at all for attractive young cousins. When he visits Mrs Bennet's sister, Mrs Philips, he confuses her with his odd combination of excessive politeness but unintentionally insulting comments. After apologizing repeatedly for intruding, he 'was so much struck with the size and furniture of the apartment, that he declared he might almost have supposed himself in the smaller summer breakfast parlour at Rosings; a comparison that did not at first convey much gratification' (p.75).

At the Netherfield Ball, with its expectation of social interaction through dance, Mr Collins is put into a setting that reveals more of his autistic traits, particularly in the areas of the coordination and timing of movements:

> Neuroscientists consider movement regulation and sensory regulation to be 'two sides of the same coin.' In fact it is not hard to imagine why individuals with movement disturbances would be seen to have difficulties in social communication and interaction, where even a small difference in behaviour can have an enormous effect. Smiling too much or too little or at the wrong time, grimacing when you mean to grin, taking ten seconds rather than the expected two seconds to respond, all can give an erroneous impression. If these problems begin early in life, obviously they will interrupt the person's ability to participate in 'the dance of relationships.' This interruption will further narrow the range of available learning experiences. (Donnellan and Robledo 2006, p.94)

Mr Collins is certainly among the group with movement disturbances as 'awkward and solemn, apologizing instead of attending, and often moving wrong without being aware of it, [he] gave [Elizabeth] all the shame and misery which a disagreeable partner for a couple of dances can give' (p.90).

But he is just as much an embarrassment off the dance floor as on it. Although in the society of that day one did not introduce oneself to a social superior, Mr Collins – upon hearing that a nephew of his patroness is present – decides to make himself known to him. Naturally Elizabeth, with her sensitive awareness of social niceties, 'tried hard to dissuade him from such a scheme... – Mr Collins listened to her with the determined air of following his own inclination' (p.97). Such rigidity once a decision has been made is often seen in those with Asperger's syndrome or high-functioning autism. 'And with a low bow he left her to attack Mr Darcy...whose astonishment at being so addressed was very evident' (pp.97–8). It may have been 'very evident' to most observers but it certainly was not to Mr Collins since, for those on the spectrum, the ability to read faces, especially rapidly in real time, is often impaired.

> Mr Darcy was eyeing him with unrestrained wonder, and when at last Mr Collins allowed him time to speak, replied with an air of distant civility. Mr Collins, however, was not discouraged from speaking again, and Mr Darcy's contempt seemed abundantly increasing with the length of his second speech, and at the end of it he only made him a slight bow, and moved another way. Mr Collins then returned to Elizabeth.
>
> 'I have no reason, I assure you,' said he, 'to be dissatisfied with my reception. Mr Darcy seemed much pleased with the attention. He answered me with the utmost civility...' (p.98)

The poorly coordinated Mr Collins manages to strike out for a third time in the evening by again lapsing into sermon mode in a social situation. He delivers a lengthy monologue on parish duties in the middle of the ball, not just to those near him but 'so loud as to be heard by half the room. – Many stared' (p.101).

Being completely oblivious that his social errors at the ball might have aroused prejudices against him, Mr Collins proceeds in his usual pompous, heavy-handed manner towards his goal of acquiring both a life partner for himself and a companion for his patroness from among his second cousins. 'Having...no feelings of diffidence to make it distressing to himself even at the moment, he set about it in a very orderly manner, with all the observances which he supposed a regular part of the business' (p.104). His self-knowledge is so strikingly limited that he says:

> 'But before I am run away with my feelings on this subject, perhaps
> it will be advisable for me to state my reasons for marrying…' The
> idea of Mr Collins, with all his solemn composure, being run away
> with by his feelings, made Elizabeth so near laughing that she could
> not use the short pause he allowed in any attempt to stop him farther
> and he continued… (p.105)

…and continued and continued and continued.

Even if Elizabeth had been composed enough to attempt to stop him,
her chances of success would have been minimal. As Dr Tony Attwood has
noted about those on the spectrum:

> Once the conversation has begun there seems to be no 'off' switch
> and it only ends when the [person's] pre-determined and practised
> 'script' is completed… The [person] appears oblivious of their effect
> on the listener even if the listener shows distinct signs of embarrass-
> ment or desire to end the interaction. (1998, p.68)

Certainly 'oblivious' has described Mr Collins in other situations and it is
appropriate again in this most sensitive one. Not only do Lizzy's facial expressions or gestures fail to register with him, but he also is not able to process her
words and intonation correctly. He dismisses her refusal as 'usual with young
ladies to reject the addresses of the man whom they secretly mean to accept',
declares himself 'by no means discouraged by what you have just said' and
assures her that he 'shall hope to lead you to the altar ere long' (p.107). Relying on reason rather than romance, he proceeds to list why he is certain that
she will ultimately marry him. He concludes by informing Lizzy that she
'should take it into further consideration that in spite of your manifold attractions, it is by no means certain that another offer of marriage may ever be
made you' (p.108). He offers this as a practical consideration without any
awareness that it is more likely to be construed as the highly insulting last
straw toppling his proposal to the ground.

Mr Collins finally understands that Elizabeth's refusal is both genuine
and final:

> He thought too well of himself to comprehend on what motives his
> cousin could refuse him; and though his pride was hurt, he suffered
> in no other way. His regard for her was quite imaginary… (p.112).

> His feelings were chiefly expressed, not by embarrassment, or
> dejection, or by trying to avoid her, but by stiffness of manner and
> resentful silence. He scarcely ever spoke to her, and the assiduous

attentions which he had been so sensible of himself, were transferred for the rest of the day to Miss Lucas... Elizabeth had hoped
that his resentment might shorten his visit, but his plan did not
appear in the least affected by it. He was always to have gone on Saturday, and to Saturday he still meant to stay. (p.115)

Mr Collins has no sense of any social or emotional awkwardness involved in
his remaining as a guest in the Bennet household after being rejected by one
of their daughters. However, in this case, his obtuseness and persistence
help him achieve his goal.

Marriage, not a particular marital partner, is his aim, so once again he
has no difficulty shifting his supposed affections to yet another: the realisti-
cally practical Charlotte Lucas, who is several years his senior.

In as short a time as Mr Collins's long speeches would allow, every
thing was settled between them to the satisfaction of both... The
stupidity with which he was favoured by nature, must guard his
courtship from any charm that could make a woman wish for its
continuance; and Miss Lucas, who accepted him solely from the
pure and disinterested desire of an establishment, cared not how
soon that establishment were gained. (pp.121–2)

This very hasty progression from meeting to marriage is not atypical of men
on the autistic spectrum. Maxine Aston, in her book *The Other Half of
Asperger Syndrome*, notes that:

Courtship with men with Asperger syndrome can be short-lived if
their sole desire is to find a wife. Often it is a need to be married that
motivates men with Asperger syndrome to seek out a partner in the
first place. If such a man believes he has found a suitable partner who
has all the qualities he is looking for, then the topic of marriage may
enter the conversation quite early on. (2001, p.31)

Austen comments rather harshly: 'Mr Collins to be sure was neither sensible
nor agreeable; his society was irksome, and his attachment to her must be
imaginary' (p.122). Poor Mr Collins, unlike many on the autistic spectrum,
does not appear to have the compensatory advantage of high intelligence to
help balance his weak social skills. Neither has the random chance of genet-
ics blessed him with an attractive face and build, nor has his environment
included the social capital of wealthy and/or caring parents. With his marriage to a woman of sense, however, his life has taken a positive turn as he
has achieved his goal. Over time, Charlotte may be able to guide him in such
a way as to reduce some of his social liabilities.

Improvements will be slight and slow so cannot all be accomplished in the early period of wedded bliss. When Elizabeth visits the newly-weds at Hunsford a mere two months after their wedding, 'she saw instantly that her cousin's manners were not altered by his marriage; his formal civility was just what it had been…as soon as they were in the parlour, he welcomed them a second time with ostentatious formality' (p.155). That he continues to talk in a way that betrays his lack of common sense or awareness of others is revealed by such observations as 'when Mr Collins said any thing of which his wife might reasonably be ashamed, which certainly was not unseldom…' (p.156).

Like many individuals with ASD, Mr Collins's fascination with numbers and patterns is very much in evidence. As he tours his visitors around, 'every view was pointed out with a minuteness which left beauty entirely behind. He could number the fields in every direction and could tell how many trees were in the most distant clump' (p.156). As the parsonage party approaches the hallowed halls of Rosings, Elizabeth:

> could not be in such raptures as Mr Collins expected the scene to inspire, and was but slightly affected by his enumeration of the windows in front of the house, and his relation of what the glazing altogether had originally cost Sir Lewis De Bourgh. (p.161)

Again numbers captivate him, so he is unaware that excessive focus on the price of the windows might be of interest to a glazier but probably not to a pair of young girls such as Elizabeth and Maria.

Attwood notes that 'a fascination with a topic' is very common in people with ASD and that they often develop 'an encyclopedic knowledge' of it. He adds that 'a common feature is a fascination with statistics, order and symmetry' (1998, p.90). Nowadays dinosaurs, sports trivia and trains are common passions but the narrowness and precision of topics is limitless.

> Many people have a hobby, and having a special interest is not in itself significant. The difference between the normal range and the eccentricity observed in Asperger's Syndrome is that the pursuits are often solitary, idiosyncratic and dominate the person's time and conversation. (Attwood 1998, p.93)

In some cases this may lead to excellent research projects and beneficial discoveries but it can be a limited asset socially unless with like-minded people such as at a gathering of coin collectors or at a *Star Trek* convention, for example. A Rosings fan club, however, is significantly limited in the breadth of its appeal. Mr Collins is likely to remain unchallenged in his self-assumed role as president!

As the parsonage party approaches the residence of the De Bourghs we see that Charlotte, through advance preparation, is starting to limit her life partner's opportunities to be socially gauche. 'Mrs Collins had settled it with her husband that the office of introduction should be her's, [therefore] it was performed in a proper manner, without any of those apologies and thanks which he would have thought necessary' (p.161).

As Lizzy's six-week stay as a guest in the Collins household draws to a close, her cousin 'took the opportunity of paying the parting civilities which he deemed indispensably necessary' (p.215). His limited *theory of mind*, or ability to see a situation from another's perspective, is evidenced once again when he completely misinterprets the high points of her visit. Lizzy, of course, has come for the pleasure of spending time with her dear and lifelong friend, Charlotte. Mr Collins overlooks that advantage to focus on his having had the:

> power to introduce you to very superior society, and from our con-
> nection with Rosings, the frequent means of varying the humble
> home scene. I think we may flatter ourselves that your Hunsford
> visit cannot have been entirely irksome. Our situation with regard to
> Lady Catherine's family is indeed the sort of extraordinary advan-
> tage and blessing which few can boast. (p.216)

Besides being unaware of what has truly appealed to Elizabeth, he is also oblivious to the differences in personality and needs between himself and his wife. That he sees her as part of himself rather than as a unique individual is conveyed by his proud boast that:

> My dear Charlotte and I have but one mind and one way of think-
> ing. There is in every thing a most remarkable resemblance of
> character and ideas between us. We seem to have been designed for
> each other. (p.216)

So Elizabeth leaves him to his partner, his patroness and his parish duties. Pity the parishioners! Even by the different standards of the time, Mr Collins lacks the ability to become a beloved shepherd of a tender flock. Rather than keeping the wolf away he frequently invites her to come as he carries the 'minutest concerns' (p.169) of his congregation to Lady Catherine De Bourgh, who then sallies forth to 'scold them into harmony and plenty' (p.169). Months earlier, at the Netherfield ball, when he had listed all that the rector of a parish had to do, concerns for the spiritual, moral and physical well-being of the people of that parish were not mentioned. He focused on money immediately, saying, 'In the first place, he must make such an agreement for tythes as may be beneficial to himself and not offensive to his patron' (p.101). Next he mentioned the writing of sermons but then combined the time for parish duties with 'the care and improvement of his dwelling' (p.101). As the crowning duty of a clergyman he stressed that he 'should have attentive and conciliatory manners towards every body, especially towards those to whom he owes his preferment' (p.101). This is a clergyman who gives 'all glory, laud and honour' to an earthly rather than heavenly lord!

Any hope that he might be an emotional support for his parishioners or others in times of deep distress is dashed by the clear example of his inability to empathize that he provides when he writes to his cousins following Lydia's elopement. Far from alleviating suffering, his words only produce more pain by pointing out the dire nature of the situation. Truly a Job's comforter! The phrases he heaps upon the family's already over-burdened shoulders include (on pp.296–7):

- 'so severe a misfortune'

- 'a circumstance which must be of all others most afflicting to a parent's mind'

- 'the death of your daughter would have been a blessing in comparison to this'

- 'you are grieviously to be pitied'

- 'for who, as Lady Catherine herself condescendingly says, will connect themselves with such a family?'

In the future, for the sake of the people of his parish, it will be best if he continues to busy himself with his garden and his bees rather than their burdens.

5

Mary Bennet

'every impulse of feeling should be guided by reason' (p.32)

Mary, the middle sister, is introduced to us when she is addressed bluntly and sarcastically by her father in the middle of a heated family discussion: 'What say you, Mary? for you are a young lady of deep reflection I know, and read great books, and make extracts' (p.7). No doubt startled by his rare attention to her, 'Mary wished to say something very sensible, but knew not how' (p.7). Is her lack of a fast response due to her wounded feelings, to a language processing disorder, or is it an immediate if subtle indication of her being on the autistic spectrum? A person with autism has been quoted as saying, 'I sometimes know in my head what the words are but they do not always come out... When I am very frightened by somebody or some-thing...I can often make motor movements and a noise, but the words just do not come out' (Joliffe, Landsdown and Robinson 1992, p.15). Whatever the cause for Mary's lack of response, what is obvious is that she is not a daughter who has endeared herself to her father. Their interest in books is in common but not shared.

When Mary does speak, she reveals that she draws her knowledge of human nature not from the lively original sources around her but through the secondary mediation of the written word.

> 'Pride,' observed Mary, who piqued herself upon the solidity of her reflections, 'is a very common failing I believe. *By all that I have ever read*, I am convinced that it is very common indeed, that human nature is particularly prone to it, and that there are very few of us who do not cherish a feeling of self-complacency on the score of some quality or other, real or imaginary...' (p.20, my italics)

Her self-awareness seems too limited for her to realize that by this statement she has just exposed in herself the self-complacency of which she speaks.

As she does for Mr Collins, Jane Austen gives us an honest but almost harsh portrait of this character she has created: 'Mary had neither genius nor taste; and though vanity had given her application, it had given her likewise a pedantic air and conceited manner, which would have injured a higher degree of excellence than she had reached' (p.25). The word 'pedantic' reveals that she shares with her second cousin, Mr Collins, this Asperger's tendency to overly formal speech.

The possibility of Mary being autistic has been raised before, in one of Joanna Brown's 'Miniatures' articles in the September 2003 edition of the magazine *Jane Austen's Regency World*. Ms Brown comments that:

> a lively discussion of Mary's talents – or otherwise – on the Austen-L list a few years ago brought up the possibility of Mary being slightly autistic. She lives in her own reality where she does not have to compete with her sisters, and is seemingly unaware of the impact she has upon people. (Brown 2003, p.39)

She certainly most obviously has the characteristics we in our century refer to as being typical of a 'nerd'. In an essay in *The Talk in Jane Austen*, Scott comments how 'Mary, unlike the other characters, talks as though she were writing. Her speeches are not so much foolish as ponderously formal' (2002, p.234). His explanation for this inappropriate communication style, however, is that she 'speaks and acts like a writer, in fact, Mary is the closest we come in this novel to having a character who stands in for Austen herself' (p.226). However, the vast majority of writers do not sound like writers when they are talking; they are aware that a much less formal style is used in conversation. Scott notes that, 'The influence of books is so strong and deep, in fact, that Mary speaks not as a speaker, but as a writer. Her speeches are lifted from books, both serious and sentimental' (p.232). All who have worked with young autistic children know that many naïve listeners have been impressed by their ability to parrot the dialogue from entire movies or repeat favourite books verbatim. However, this is merely a form of speech called echolalia, as they often do not understand what they have just said nor can they paraphrase it in their own words.

As the middle child, Mary, is in an isolated position in her family with no one who can pull her into their social world. Jane and Lizzy form the older, sensible pair while Kitty and Lydia are the younger, silly duo. Mary makes no effort to be included in either pairing, often turning down what invitations they do extend to her to join them. As Scott astutely notes, 'she is consistently unsocial, and often very nearly antisocial, in a novel that is taken up entirely with social issues and situations' (2002, p.229). Her parents ignore or reject her without recognizing her high needs for social modelling and guidance. Her natural tendency to turn to the certainty of books is increased by the lack of any obvious alternatives for companionship within her family.

Mary's reaction to Jane's illness clearly indicates how much she distrusts emotion and values the intellect: 'I admire the activity of your benevolence…but every impulse of feeling should be guided by reason' (p.32), she states to Elizabeth who is about to walk three miles to Netherfield due to her concern for their eldest sister's well-being. Dr Temple Grandin, in her book about her life as an autistic person, comments that, 'I still have difficulty understanding and having a relationship with people whose primary motivation in life is governed by complex emotions, as my actions are guided by intellect' (1995, p.90). She continues, 'it was years before I realized that other people are guided by their emotions during most social interactions' (p.95).

Some days after Jane's recovery, following the supper at the ball at Netherfield, Mary, 'after very little entreaty', prepares to sing although, in Elizabeth's opinion, her 'powers were by no means fitted for such a display; her voice was weak, and her manner affected' (p.100). Attempting to prevent her family from further disgracing themselves and thereby her, Elizabeth tries to signal her sister to decline. 'By many significant looks and silent entreaties, did she endeavour to prevent such a proof of complaisance, – but in vain; Mary would not understand them' (p.100).

Would not? Or could not? I do not feel that Mary is choosing to ignore her sister; rather, as a person on the autistic spectrum, she is not able to read facial expressions quickly. Ashley Stanford, in her book *Asperger Syndrome and Long-term Relationships*, shares her realization of how little information her husband, a computer programmer, was able to get from looking at her face. When she described for him what she could tell about people from their facial expressions she noted:

> It's highly likely that he thought I was making it all up. Reading information in a person's eyes and face is as foreign to him as his programming code is to me…at least now I realize that he isn't receiving the many messages my eyes are sending. I can't be angry with him for not receiving messages that he cannot see. (2003, p.74)

Mary has some interest in attracting positive attention but sadly knows not how. Of the five sisters she is the only one who may have welcomed the attentions of Mr Collins but, unlike Charlotte, she does not know how to respond quickly and empathetically when the position as his bride becomes vacant after his rejection by Elizabeth.

> Mary might have been prevailed upon to accept him. She rated his abilities much higher than any of the others; there was a solidity in his reflections which often struck her, and though by no means so clever as herself, she thought that if encouraged to read and improve himself by such an example as hers, he might become a very agreeable companion. (p.124)

This attraction between fictional characters with an autistic spectrum disorder has been replicated countless times in real life. During her research Maxine Aston found that:

> most of the women [she] spoke to with Asperger syndrome were in relationships with men who also had Asperger syndrome. This was very different from the men with Asperger syndrome, the majority of whom had formed a relationship with an NT [neuro-typical] woman. (2003, p.178)

Scott interprets Mary's positive regard for Mr Collins as showing that she is 'a surprisingly compassionate person' (2002, p.227). However, as we have seen, she shows little compassion or concern when Jane is ill nor, later in the book, is she truly empathetic to Elizabeth after Lydia's elopement. I feel that her regard for Mr Collins is more a case of like minds being attracted to each other. Mary is not able to see how socially gauche he is any more than she recognizes her own limited connectedness to those around her.

Mary exhibits further autistic traits at a time of major emotional turmoil when her youngest sister, Lydia, runs off with Wickham. When her elder sisters return to Longbourn they are 'soon joined by Mary and Kitty...the faces of both, however, were tolerably calm; and no change was visible in either'. Mary, 'with a countenance of grave reflection', whispers to Lizzy: 'This is a most unfortunate affair; and will probably be much talked of. But we must stem the tide of malice, and pour into the wounded bosoms of each other, the balm of sisterly consolation' (p.289).

Unfortunately, although she knows at the abstract level that sisters should comfort each other, she has no idea of how to go about it. Neither by

gesture nor facial expression does she actually provide empathy and consolation. Words flow however:

> Then, perceiving in Elizabeth no inclination of replying, she added,
> 'Unhappy as the event must be for Lydia, we may draw from it this
> useful lesson; that loss of virtue in a female is irretrievable – that one
> false step involves her in endless ruin – that her reputation is no less
> brittle than it is beautiful – and that she cannot be too much guarded
> in her behaviour towards the undeserving of the other sex.'
>
> Elizabeth lifted up her eyes in amazement, but was too much
> oppressed to make any reply. Mary, however, continued to console
> herself with such kind of moral extractions from the evil before
> them. (p.289)

Mary is unable to recognize from Elizabeth's facial expression and silence
that her moralizing platitudes are bruising her further rather than acting as
the 'balm of sisterly consolation' she knew she should offer. Temple
Grandin describes numerous examples of other autistic people who, like
Mary, have trouble knowing how to respond appropriately. She mentions a
man with autism who had an 'intellectual awareness of how other people
felt, but he did not experience those feelings himself [and a woman who]
described how she copied emotions so that she acted normal, but it was a
purely mechanical process, like retrieving files from a computer' (1995,
p.135).

After the marriages of three of the Bennet sisters, Jane Austen tells us
that 'Mary was obliged to mix more with the world' because of 'Mrs
Bennet's being quite unable to sit alone' (p.386). Rather harshly, her previous retreat from the world is blamed on her awareness that she was the least
attractive physically of the sisters; since 'as she was no longer mortified by
comparisons between her sisters' beauty and her own, it was suspected by
her father that she submitted to the change without much reluctance'
(p.386). However, her father, who has neglected her throughout her life, is
far from being the best judge of her motivations or feelings.

Earlier in the book we have been told that Mary, 'in consequence of
being the only plain one in the family, worked hard for knowledge and
accomplishments' (p.25). However, I propose that her passion for books and
study reflects her intelligent and autistic nature, not just a desire to shine in a
different area from her sisters. Mary does not seem either to value or be
aware of the value her society placed on feminine beauty. She actually seems
quite self-confident in the scenes in which she appears in the book (the films

are a different matter). Scott perceptively commented about her that she 'does not speak easily or very well because speech is a social activity…and she does not know how to play that game well; she really doesn't care to' (2002, p.236). As a person with mild to moderate autism, Mary would generally be unaware that other people valued different things than she did herself.

If Mary did not object too strongly to being obliged to be with her mother more, it may have been that she found it more manageable to have just one other woman to relate to rather than five. The noise, bustle and undertones of undecipherable meaning in the intact Bennet household must have been quite overwhelming for her. The ricocheting speed of conversation in a verbal, lively group can be particularly challenging for some people whose high-functioning autistic traits include subtle language-processing problems. They will say that they 'can't keep up'.

In our century, Mary would be able to find a niche in life much more compatible to her talents than merely keeping her mother company. She possesses the intelligence, self-motivation and ability to focus that could lead her into a satisfying career in fields such as research or computer technology. The tragedy of her life is not her looks but rather her lack of suitable options to make use of her abilities.

6

Lydia Bennet

'untamed, unabashed, wild, noisy, and fearless' (p.315)

Lydia bursts into the novel and our attention without waiting for more than a cursory introduction. During the Bennet ladies' visit to Netherfield, ostentatiously to enquire after Jane's health, when her mother orders their carriage:

> the youngest of her daughters put herself forward. The two girls had been whispering to each other during the whole visit, and the result of it was, that the youngest should tax Mr Bingley with having promised on his first coming into the country to give a ball at Netherfield.
>
> Lydia was a stout, well-grown girl of fifteen, with a fine complexion and good-humoured countenance; a favourite with her mother, whose affection had brought her into public at an early age. She had high animal spirits, and a sort of natural self-consequence, which the attentions of the officers...had increased into assurance. She was very equal therefore to address Mr Bingley on the subject of the ball, and abruptly reminded him of his promise; adding, that it would be the most shameful thing in the world if he did not keep it. (p.45)

In this encounter, by her blunt introduction of a new topic and her disregard for the social mores that should prevent her from speaking in so chiding a manner to an older man whom she has just met, Lydia shows signs of having poorly developed social skills. The reference to her 'high animal spirits' indicates other concerns that make her a challenging daughter and sister. Soon after, when once again meeting a new and older man, Mr Collins, Lydia also interrupts him with an abrupt topic change. While he is reading a sermon aloud, she interjects speculation about her uncle's dismissal of a servant.

Her tendency to dominate a conversation with an excited monologue about her own interests is apparent early on as well. During party games at her aunt and uncle's home in Meryton, 'she was a most determined talker' (p.76). Her impulsiveness and difficulty maintaining her focus, even on such a new and attractive source of interest as Mr Wickham, are exposed when 'being likewise extremely fond of lottery tickets, she soon grew too much interested in the game, too eager in making bets and exclaiming after prizes, to have attention for any one in particular' (p.76).

Attention and the control of it are not traits that Lydia has among her abundant charms. As the Bennet family group return in the carriage from the supper party at their relatives' home:

> neither Lydia nor Mr Collins were once silent. Lydia talked inces-
> santly of lottery tickets, of the fish she had lost and the fish she had
> won, and Mr Collins, in describing the civility of Mr and Mrs
> Philips, protesting that he did not in the least regard his losses at
> whist, enumerating all the dishes at supper, and repeatedly fearing
> that he crouded his cousins, had more to say that he could well man-
> age before the carriage stopped at Longbourn House. (p.84)

Two parallel monologues in one vehicle; two peas in a pod. Although her autistic tendencies are packaged in a more attractive exterior than that possessed by poor Mr Collins, they have some remarkable similarities. How shocked Lydia would be to be told that!

As our acquaintance with Lydia increases we for a third time see her interrupt an older male. When Sir William Lucas is sharing the news of his daughter's sudden engagement, 'Lydia, always unguarded and often uncivil, boisterously exclaimed, "Good Lord! Sir William, how can you tell such a story?"' (p.126).

When Lydia organizes a luncheon to welcome Elizabeth and Jane home from London, she relates a long, rather risqué tale about dressing up one of the soldiers in women's clothes:

> Lydia, in a voice rather louder than any other person's, was enumer-
> ating the various pleasures of the morning to any body who would
> hear her.
>
> 'Oh! Mary,' said she, 'I wish you had gone with us, for we had
> such fun as we went along, Kitty and me drew up all the blinds...

And then we were so merry all the way home! We talked and
laughed so loud, that any body might have heard us ten miles off!'

To this, Mary very gravely replied, '...I should infinitely prefer
a book.'

But of this answer Lydia heard not a word. She seldom listened
to any body for more than half a minute, and never attended to
Mary at all. (pp.222–3)

The inability to modulate the volume of her voice to match those around her
is typical of many on the autistic spectrum. In addition, the difficulty listening
and the extreme boisterousness are possible indications of attention deficit
hyperactivity disorder (ADHD). As Attwood has observed, 'Asperger's
Syndrome and Attention Deficit Disorder are two distinct conditions but it
is possible for a [person] to have both' (1998, p.146). With Lydia one gets
the uneasy feeling that anything is possible!

If indications of her potentially dual diagnosis are apparent in this luncheon incident, they are even more blatant when Lydia is invited to go to
Brighton with the commander of the militia, Colonel Forster, and his young
bride:

> The rapture of Lydia on this occasion, her adoration of Mrs Forster,
> the delight of Mrs Bennet, and the mortification of Kitty, are
> scarcely to be described. Wholly inattentive to her sister's feelings,
> Lydia flew about the house in restless ecstasy, calling for every one's
> congratulations, and laughing and talking with more violence than
> ever... (p.230)

She completely disregards the feelings of overwhelming disappointment
expressed by her next-in-age sister, Kitty, who, throughout their lives, has
been her constant companion. This inability even to notice another's emotion let alone empathize with it supports the diagnosis of ASD, while the
'restless ecstasy' and 'talking with more violence than ever' are strong indicators of the ADHD diagnosis.

As usual it is Elizabeth who is most observant of all the family members,
hence most aware both of the severity of Lydia's difficulties and of how vulnerable, despite her self-confidence, they make her. Using very strong language she attempts to convince their father that there is cause for alarm and
that Lydia must be protected from herself. The words she uses to describe
her youngest sister include (on p.231):

- 'Lydia's unguarded and imprudent manner'

- 'the wild volatility, the assurance and disdain for all restraint which mark Lydia's character'

- 'vain, ignorant, idle, and absolutely uncontrolled!'

Lizzy, therefore, is one of the few members of the family not to be taken completely off guard by the news that Lydia has disgraced them all by running off with Wickham. Regarding her youngest sister she 'had no difficulty in believing that neither her virtue nor her understanding would preserve her from falling an easy prey' (p.280). She is correct in recognizing that her sister's 'understanding' puts her at risk in that 'vulnerability is often apparent in children and adolescents with Asperger syndrome… due to the inability to put themselves into another's mind, and see another's motives, they cannot always figure out when they are being lied to or used' (Aston 2003, p.27). Lizzy recalls that her sister's 'affections had been continually fluctuating, but never without an object' (p.280). Like the distant cousin she despises, the recipients of Lydia's affections have been interchangeable. While in the course of a few days Mr Collins contemplated marriage in turn with Jane, then Elizabeth and finally Charlotte, Lydia's 'love' also has tripped from one youthful target to another as she reacts only to the red coat not to the uniqueness of the individual wearing it. This lack of emotional depth is a frequent indicator of an autistic spectrum disorder. Although many people with Asperger's have an academic passion, Lydia's passion is for 'passion' itself (or at least the martial appearance of it). As Lizzy despairingly tells Aunt Gardiner about her youngest sister, 'Since the –shire were first quartered in Meryton, nothing but love, flirtation, and officers, have been in her head' (p.284).

If eloping reveals Lydia's obliviousness to the social and moral standards of her day, then her amusement in telling of it betrays her equal obliviousness to the feelings of others. In her departing letter to Harriet Forster she gleefully assures her friend that:

> You need not send them word at Longbourn of my going, if you do not like it, for it will make the surprise the greater, when I write to them, and sign my name Lydia Wickham. What a good joke it will be! I can hardly write for laughing… (p.291)

When Lizzy reads this she cries out, 'Oh! Thoughtless, thoughtless Lydia!' However, in this case, it is not so much lack of thought as it is *lack of feeling* that is the crux of her problem.

The same limited awareness of the thoughts and feelings of others is apparent even after Lydia has achieved the (in her case dubious) status of married woman. Marriage has not gifted her with maturity of thought or behaviour. When she returns to Longbourn with her husband, despite the change of surname, 'Lydia was Lydia still; untamed, unabashed, wild, noisy, and fearless. She turned from sister to sister, demanding their congratulations…' (p.315). Those most aware of the awkwardness of the situation were the two who had done the least to cause it: Elizabeth 'blushed, and Jane blushed; but the cheeks of the two who caused their confusion, suffered no variation of colour' (p.316).

Given the individuals involved there was no need to fear an uncomfortable silence. 'There was no want of discourse. The bride and her mother could neither of them talk fast enough…and Lydia led voluntarily to subjects, which her sisters would not have alluded to for the world' (p.316). Elizabeth tries to communicate to her sister the inappropriateness of her remarks as she 'looked expressively at Lydia; but she, who never heard nor saw anything of which she chose to be insensible, gaily continued…' (p.316). However, as a person with ASD, Lydia's inability to read and react to a message sent with the eyes is not a choice but rather a true lack of ability to be sensible/sensitive to it. There is a genuine failure to comprehend that the eyes convey information. Lorna Wing quotes a person with Asperger's syndrome as realizing that 'people give each other messages with their eyes but I do not know what they are saying' (1992, p. 131).

Continued exposure to her eldest sisters and their reproaches, whether silent or otherwise, does nothing to make Lydia see her elopement in anything but a positive light: 'It was not to be supposed that time would give Lydia that embarrassment, from which she had been so wholly free at first. Her ease and good spirits increased' (p.317). With complacency rather than irony Lydia announces, 'I am sure my sisters must all envy me' (p.317).

There is great irony, although again unintentionally so on her part, when the following exchange between Lydia and her second sister occurs:

> 'Lizzy, I never gave *you* an account of my wedding, I believe. You were not by, when I told mamma, and the others, all about it. Are not you curious to hear how it was managed?'

> 'No really,' replied Elizabeth; 'I think there cannot be too little said on the subject.'
>
> 'La! You are so strange!' (p.318)

This extraordinary confidence that her own point of view is the only one possible is typical of some on the spectrum. Lydia has no conception that the majority would feel that it is she, rather than her sensitive sister, who is the strange one.

Despite Elizabeth's clearly declared lack of interest, Lydia wishes to tell her the details, so tell her she does. Once decided on a plan of action, shifting plans is a challenge for anyone with ASD. Lydia launches into an account of the preparations for her wedding and by that telling reveals once again how her mind becomes fixated on minutiae while missing the main point. A tiny detail of the wedding rather than the life-changing immensity of marriage is uppermost in her mind, despite the best efforts of a wiser woman. Lydia relates:

> And there was my aunt, all the time I was dressing, preaching and talking away just as if she was reading a sermon. However, I did not hear above one word in ten, for I was thinking, you may suppose, of my dear Wickham. I longed to know whether he would be married in his blue coat. (p.319)

It is the colour of the coat not the character of the groom that is paramount to this bride.

As Lydia continues on with her re-telling, she demonstrates yet again her complete inability to judge her situation from anyone else's perspective. She is not only genuinely shocked by what she views as the unjustifiable strictness of her aunt and uncle but assumes that Elizabeth will be also. Resentfully she recalls, 'my uncle and aunt were horrid unpleasant all the time I was with them… Not one party, or scheme, or any thing' (p.319). No doubt, in Lydia's view, they are 'strange' as well.

Once Lydia has launched into her oft-told monologue about her wedding she is not able to monitor its suitability for this particular audience. On and on she goes until out spills the information that Mr Darcy had accompanied Wickham to the wedding. This disclosure is so major that even Lydia realizes that she has committed a transgression and gasps, 'But gracious me! I quite forgot! I ought not to have said a word about it. I promised them so faithfully… It was to be such a secret !' (p.319). When Jane and Elizabeth respond that if it is a secret they will ask no questions, Lydia's response exhibits the honesty and difficulty with subterfuge that is one of the more positive traits associated with being on the spectrum. In order to lie you have to understand how someone else thinks so that you know how to trick them. Lydia does not possess such complex insight into another's mind so lying is not numbered among her many failings. She reacts with relief to the promise of no questions, saying with genuine honesty, 'for if you did [ask], I should certainly tell you all' (p.320).

Although she refrains from questioning Lydia, Elizabeth naturally seeks out a more reliable source in her Aunt Gardiner. Her prompt response, besides containing much information for Lizzy to ponder, also confirms the impressions we have of Lydia. Her lack of emotional depth is emphasized once again when we are told that appeals for better behaviour based on the desire to be accepted by others were to no avail. She responded negatively to her aunt's entreaties, saying that 'she cared for none of her friends' (p.332). Even her ties to her closest sister, Kitty, and to her recent bosom friend, Harriet, are lightly discarded.

Aunt Gardiner's description of the behaviour of her youngest niece confirms Lydia's dual challenges of autism, with its limited empathy for others, and of attention deficit disorder, with its difficulty focusing on what is being said:

> I would not tell you how little I was satisfied with *her* behaviour while she staid with us, if I had not perceived, by Jane's letter last Wednesday, that her conduct on coming home was exactly of a piece with it, and therefore what I now tell you, can give you no fresh pain. I talked to her repeatedly in the most serious manner, representing to her all the wickedness of what she had done, and all the unhappiness she had brought on her family. If she heard me, it was by good luck, for I am sure she did not listen. (p.325)

Indeed Lydia probably listened no more closely to her Aunt Gardiner than we do to a pesky fly we swat away from the sweet treat with which we are about to indulge ourselves!

The most telling example of Lydia's lack of emotional reciprocity occurs when she rides off in glory out of the main action of the novel. At barely 16 years of age she is about to leave her mother and her childhood home for an undetermined period of time that 'was likely to continue at least a twelvemonth' (p.330). If anything could melt her armour of obliviousness it would surely be the tears of her mother at this wrenching moment. Think of how our own well up whether facing such a break ourselves or simply in sympathy when we witness intense emotion at train stations and airports. But it doesn't bother the former Miss Lydia Bennet in the slightest:

> 'Oh! my dear Lydia,' [her mother] cried, 'when shall we meet again?'
> 'Oh, lord! I don't know. Not these two or three years perhaps.'
> (p.330)

Such a daughter! With her dual disorders she would be an exhausting and challenging handful for even the most skilled, sensitive, devoted and energetic parents to raise. And, of course, such traits, especially sensitivity, are most noticeably lacking in her father and mother.

7

Mr Bennet

'so odd a mixture of quick parts, sarcastic humour, reserve, and caprice' (p.5)

Although most readers would agree that Mr Bennet, like the majority of us, has neither the skills nor the energy needed to parent such a complex challenge as Lydia, he has often been credited with many positive traits. He has been viewed by some as wise and witty; a philosopher who is above the materialism of his wife. The one failing that many have acknowledged is that long ago he made such a poor choice of life partner. Pity has been felt for all that the poor man has had to bear due to that one youthful mistake.

Have we been feeling sorry for the wrong person? What if some of his oft-quoted, humorous remarks are not intentionally so? What if he actually means them?

Let us re-read the justly famous exchange at the beginning of the novel, between the Bennets about the arrival of Mr Bingley in the neighbourhood:

MRS BENNET: 'A single man of large fortune; four or five thousand a year. What a fine thing for our girls!'

MR BENNET: 'How so? how can it affect them?' (p.4)

Is Mr Bennet deliberately being funny or is he expressing what he feels – mystification? What if he truly makes no connection between his wife's two sentences? Difficulty with drawing inferences and 'reading between the lines' is common among the majority of those on the spectrum.

After all, at no other time in the novel does he seem to take seriously his daughters' need to marry, even though matrimony is one of the few sources of 'employment' for ladies of his time. If we take the same verbal exchange and turn it into a conversation between a couple with five unemployed daughters living on his non-transferable pension in a present-day economically depressed area, then a response such as his would not be viewed as witty but rather as callous, unthinking and lacking in common sense:

'A factory with job openings; paying forty or fifty thousand dollars a year. What a fine thing for our girls!'

'How so? how can it affect them?'

When his wife's reply includes the phrase 'nonsense, how can you talk so!' (p.4), she is showing a much more practical awareness of the realities of life than he is. She tries to help him see the connection that is obvious to all their neighbours, like the Lucas family and the Longs, with unmarried/unemployed females: 'But consider your daughters. Only think what an establishment it would be for one of them' (p.4).

But considering his daughters is exactly what he has never done. As an extraordinarily selfish and self-centred man, Mr Bennet, throughout his married and parenting years, has thought mainly of his own comfort and interests. When he does pay any attention to his family it is for amusement and to reinforce his own sense of intellectual superiority over them. Repeatedly throughout the novel he shows that he is rarely able to see a situation from anyone else's point of view. Also, like many people on the autistic spectrum, he shows difficulty with *central coherence*, or knowing what is meaningful and important to attend to. He is better able to pay attention to details than to see connections or 'the big picture'.

Readers have often felt relieved that in her father Lizzy has at least had one parent who treasures her as she truly deserves. But how has he cared for this treasure and for the four other young lives that have blessed his marriage? Very poorly indeed.

Children need both emotional and physical nurturing. They need to be loved, but they also need to be cared for and educated in such a way as to equip them for their adulthood. Given the limited options for any women of the Regency period and the even narrower ones for 'ladies' there were three things that Mr Bennet could have done for his daughters. A truly caring, thoughtful father of five such different girls would have tried to accomplish all three but Mr Bennet made no effort to do even one!

In order to secure his daughters' well-being in adulthood Mr Bennet's three strategies could have been to give them the opportunities to acquire:

1. Wealth – so that they would be independent of others

2. Education – so that they could support themselves respectably as governesses

3. Husbands – so that they could be honourably supported by another.

When Mrs Bennet excitedly announces that an eligible bachelor has joined their small social circle she is letting her husband know that the third possibility may unexpectedly be available for one of their girls. Although they have not been taken to where the bachelors gather, miraculously, one has come to them. Mr Bennet has done nothing to provide their daughters with the standard opportunities to meet more unmarried men than exist among the local 'four and twenty families' (p.43) with whom they dine. The Bennets never went to London even though being present during the social season was considered crucial for exposing young persons of marriageable age to a wide range of others in their social class. They have not been taken because, as Elizabeth later tells Lady Catherine, 'my father hates London' (p.164). It is the rare parent that hasn't realized very early on that parenting does not consist of doing only what you like. It is also ironic that it is probably due to this dislike of leaving his own home that Mr Bennet ended up marrying the local attorney's daughter rather than someone farther afield of his own social class.

If Mr Bennet has made no attempt to bring his daughters to the attention of potential partners he has also put no effort into either of the other two options for their futures. The same trips to London would have given them 'the benefit of masters' (p.164) to develop their artistic and musical skills in order to qualify them to be governesses in affluent homes. However, the Bennets barely provided a basic education let alone any extras. Lady Catherine De Bourgh, rarely as it is possible to agree with her, is speaking the truth when she exclaims:

> No governess! How was that possible? Five daughters brought up at home without a governess! – I never heard of such a thing... Without a governess you must have been neglected. (pp.164–5)

Although Lizzy responds that 'such of us as wished to learn, never wanted the means' (p.165) and local teachers for some accomplishments were provided, it still remains that a systematic programme of instruction was not. Although aged only 15 and 17 Lydia and Kitty are not occupied in any sort of educational tasks that would equip them if they needed to earn their own livings.

Mr Bennet has also made no attempt to provide the first option of financial self-sufficiency. He and his wife, who 'had no turn for economy' (p.308), had always spent his whole income without laying by an annual sum in savings for the future. Over 20 years before, this had not seemed to be an extravagant thing to do:

> When first Mr Bennet had married, economy was held to be per-
> fectly useless; for, of course, they were to have a son. This son was to
> join in cutting off the entail, as soon as he came of age, and the
> widow and younger children would by that means be provided for.
> Five daughters successively entered the world, but yet the son was to
> come… This event had at last been despaired of, but it was then too
> late to be saving. (p. 308)

Once settled on a plan of action, or rather inaction, Mr Bennet had continued with it for several decades despite the births of a series of female
children who made the need to provide for them a matter of fact not theory.
The Bennets' financial planning had continued to be of the 'when we have a
son/win the lottery' variety. However, 15 years have passed since they last
conceived a child. Surely with five daughters in hand versus a son in the
bush Mr Bennet might have changed his strategy sooner. This rigidity and
difficulty shifting ideas is a trait often seen in autistic individuals.

His lack of forethought for his daughters' future physical well-being is
extremely serious and neglectful, but his callousness towards most of them
emotionally is equally damaging. Discussing the very deep and negative
effects that can result from having a parent with an autistic spectrum disorder, Dr Attwood observes:

> It can ruin the childhood of their ordinary kids who resent their lack
> of love and affection; they're very black and white in which kids
> they like and don't like and one kid can have total adulation and the
> other one they just don't want to know. (2000, pp. 16–17)

There are numerous examples of Mr Bennet's sweepingly critical and
derogatory statements about his three younger daughters within their hearing, beginning in the first scene when he says: 'They have none of them
much to recommend them…they are all silly and ignorant like other girls;
but Lizzy has something more of quickness than her sisters' (p. 5).

However, poor parenting and planning skills are not sufficient alone to
indicate that Mr Bennet is on the autistic spectrum. Jane Austen has given us
a masterful portrayal of this man, who is 'so odd a mixture of quick parts,
sarcastic humour, reserve, and caprice, that the experience of three and
twenty years had been insufficient to make his wife understand his character' (p. 5). In the 200 years since he was created we readers have not necessarily done much better, so we can hardly fault poor Mrs Bennet!

In the very first conversation in the novel Mr Bennet breaks the basic unwritten rule that a conversation involves reciprocal response or turn-taking.

> 'My dear Mr Bennet,' said his lady to him one day, 'have you heard that Netherfield Park is let at last?'
> Mr Bennet replied that he had not.
> 'But it is,' returned she; 'for Mrs Long has just been here and she told me all about it.'
> Mr Bennet made no answer. (p.3)

He made no answer. This seemingly insignificant short sentence is our first inkling that this man has serious social shortcomings. There are many and more blatant examples throughout the book but the signs are immediately put before us; not the first time he opens his mouth, but rather the second time he *should* have. Dr Peter Denny, Professor Emeritus in the Psychology Department of the University of Western Ontario, in response to my presentation to the JASNA branch in his city in March 2005, recalled that, '[w]hen teaching anthropological linguistics, [he had] often used this conversation…as an excellent example of failure to comply with H.P. Grice's main rule of conversation, that one must cooperate with the other person'. However, he said that, until hearing my talk about autism, he had never known any reason *why* Mr Bennet failed to extend this basic courtesy.

As many of us know, Mr Bennet does eventually bestir himself to visit the new tenant of Netherfield Park and so sets into action the events that have entranced readers for approximately two centuries. When he finally lets his wife know of his visit, a 'tumult of joy' (p.7) is unleashed. Generally in marriage, when we have managed to truly delight our partners, we bask in the resulting good feelings and 'brownie points'. However, after only one speech of praise from Mrs Bennet, in which she hails him as a loving father and declares his reticence about his true intentions to be a joke, Mr Bennet 'left the room, fatigued with the raptures of his wife' (p.8). In his classic description of those with Asperger's syndrome Tony Attwood makes reference to how some 'can be very uncomfortable when others show emotional arousal…it's almost as though they want everyone to have a flat affect'(2000, p.43).

Mr Bennet shows repeatedly that he is a man of such 'flat affect', or limited expression of the wide emotional range. For example, when Jane, who has been ill, and Elizabeth, his favourite child, return from their stay at

Netherfield Hall, their father, although 'really glad to see them', was 'very laconic in his expressions of pleasure'(p.60).

Earlier on, following the assembly, for a second time he produces yet another of the lines that is very funny unless you consider the possibility that he didn't intend it to be. Is he deliberately joking or is he actually betraying how totally self-centred he is? When his wife tries to connect him with his family's world by telling him of Mr Bingley's honouring their eldest with more dances than anyone else, she is interrupted: '"If he had had any compassion for *me*," cried her husband impatiently, "he would not have danced half so much!"' (p.13). Notice that Austen uses the adverb 'impatiently' not 'jokingly'. Mr Bennet truly has no patience with information that he cannot relate to himself. He takes no pleasure in hearing of the pleasures of others, even if they are his closest relations. The italics on the word 'me' were put there by the author herself. This emphasis draws our attention to how extraordinarily self-centred and inwardly focused Mr Bennet is. The children of such a parent are not guided and protected as they deserve.

Mrs Bennet, although cut off rudely by her husband, does manage to relate 'with much bitterness of spirit and some exaggeration, the shocking rudeness of Mr Darcy' (p.16) and to end her comments with the desire that, 'I wish you had been there, my dear, to have given him one of your set downs' (p.16). Therein lies a key point: Mr Bennet wasn't there! What was the father of five very young women doing sitting at home reading a book when, by all the social standards of the time, he should have been acting as their escort and chaperone? Historically, a watchful father, by his mere presence, lets other men know that his daughters are not to be trifled with. Mr Bennet's inability to provide that care for his daughters leads very directly to Lydia's ruin, thus providing us with 'a frightening exemplar of the perils of detachment' (Halperin 1989, p.42).

Shortly thereafter, the arrival of a third young bachelor, Mr Collins, into the limited social circle of Longbourn further reveals Mr Bennet's inability to consider the needs, let alone the wishes, of others. Although he has known for a month of the proposed visit from his heir, he has seen no need to share this information with his wife until the very morning of the young man's arrival. Most hostesses, no matter what their standard of housekeeping, prefer significantly more warning than this in order to prepare for guests.

When Mr Bennet does get around to mentioning his heir's imminent arrival he does so in an incredibly callous manner, saying that the letter is 'from my cousin, Mr Collins, who, when I am dead, may turn you all out of this house as he pleases' (p.61). This is not wit or humour; this is the truth. A painful, chilling truth presented in an uncaring manner to six women by the man who should have been the most caring towards them. Homelessness is never a joke and homelessness is literally what they would face when he died. A recent newspaper article in the *Vancouver Sun* (2 September 2006) reported that a phobia named 'bag lady syndrome' is rife even among the financially independent women of today. It was reported that it 'was found to plague 46 per cent of women in a US survey recently released by Allianz Life Insurance'. If almost half of modern women, despite both their ability to earn their own living and the underpinnings of our social services safety net, still fear ending up destitute, then consider how much more reason Mrs Bennet had in Regency England.

Thus far in the book we have seen Mr Bennet avoid social situations and new people, but now he cannot as the stranger is literally at his door and must be invited in. Despite being the host and a learned man with a reputation for wit, Mr Bennet frequently does not take his part in the conversation. We read that 'Mr Bennet indeed said little' (p.64) and that 'during dinner, Mr Bennet scarcely spoke at all' (p.66). 'Small talk and polite chitchat can be very difficult for the AS adult, as it often requires that the person speaking pretends to be interested in the other person' (Aston 2003, p.79). Thinking of, then initiating a topic that the other might enjoy discussing can be major challenges for an individual on the autistic spectrum.

Although Mr Bennet is amused by Mr Collins, he tires of company very quickly. He sends his guest off to accompany four of his daughters to Meryton as:

> he was most anxious to get rid of him, and have his library to himself; for thither Mr Collins had followed him after breakfast... Such doings discomposed Mr Bennet exceedingly. In his library he had always been sure of leisure and tranquility. (p.71)

The retreat to the library of an individual on the autistic spectrum is replayed daily in schools around the world. As Attwood noted, 'at school lunchtimes, the [student] is often found on his own or...in the library reading about their particular interest' (1998, p.31). The fact that having someone come into his library was so upsetting to Mr Bennet exemplifies another observation of Dr Attwood's, that for those 'with Asperger's

Syndrome the most stressful activity is having to socialize...[therefore it is] necessary to have islands of solitude throughout the day' (1998, p.155).

Although he usually avoids social situations Mr Bennet does attend the ball at Netherfield. For once, Elizabeth's attempts to communicate with her family by facial expression and eye gaze are semi-successful. When Mary shows no signs of taking notice of her indications that she is singing for too long, Elizabeth:

> looked at her father to entreat his interference, lest Mary should be singing all night. He took the hint, and when Mary had finished her second song, said aloud, 'That will do extremely well, child. You have delighted us long enough. Let the other young ladies have time to exhibit.' Mary, though pretending not to hear, was somewhat disconcerted; and Elizabeth sorry for her, and sorry for her father's speech, was afraid her anxiety had done no good. (pp.100–1)

Although her father stopped her sister from further embarrassing the family he did so in an abrupt, insensitive way that only drew additional negative attention to them. For the rest of the evening he observes his family with detached amusement, with no sense of embarrassment, as he is oblivious to the fact that, in the eyes of the majority in their patriarchal society, their behaviour must reflect poorly on him as the head of the household.

Back at Longbourn, despite the presence of a house guest, Mr Bennet lets nothing interfere with his established routines. Once again he is to be found in the library, quite oblivious to the momentous events around him. When his wife bursts through the door in a state of alarm that Lizzy has rejected Mr Collins's offer of marriage, 'Mr Bennet raised his eyes from his book as she entered, and fixed them on her face with a calm unconcern which was not in the least altered by her communication' (p.110). Generally our faces mirror the emotions of those talking to us, but Mr Bennet is unable to show or feel any empathy to his wife in her distress. A man of more emotional depth would manage both to uphold Elizabeth's right to decide and at the same time show sympathy for his wife's great disappointment that this rare opportunity for future security was being rejected. Mr Bennet shows no awareness of his wife's feelings and concerns. Instead his comments to her focus on himself as he asks that she respect *his* intelligence and *his* need for privacy:

> I have two small favours to request. First, that you will allow me the free use of my understanding on the present occasion; and secondly,

of my room. I shall be glad to have the library to myself as soon as may be. (p.112)

As readers we have been so delighted that he supported Elizabeth that we have overlooked the fact that he did not extend the same courtesy and support to his wife.

Similarly, when the engagement of Mr Collins to Charlotte Lucas is announced only days later, Mr Bennet is oblivious to the very real distress of his wife. Understandably, 'Mrs Bennet was really in a most pitiable state' (p.129) at this now irretrievable loss of what had been the best opportunity for marriage/security yet to be offered to one of their daughters.

> The very mention of any thing concerning the match threw her into an agony of ill humour, and wherever she went she was sure of hearing it talked of... Whenever Charlotte came to see them she concluded her to be anticipating the hour of possession; and whenever she spoke in a low voice to Mr Collins, was convinced that they were talking of the Longbourn estate, and resolving to turn herself and her daughters out of the house, as soon as Mr Bennet were dead. (p.130)

Her husband's response is again to make fun of her very realistic fears of homelessness as he responds sarcastically, 'My dear, do not give way to such gloomy thoughts. Let us hope for better things. Let us flatter ourselves that *I* may be the survivor.' As Jane Austen notes, 'This was not very consoling to Mrs Bennet' (p.130). Indeed it is far from comforting to be told that the most positive alternative to the lack of a roof over your head is the lid of a casket!

Many feel that Mrs Bennet's lack of intellect and frequent hysteria have triggered her husband's callousness towards her. In my opinion this is a variation on the old theme of 'she asked for it', which is no longer tolerated in cases of physical abuse; it does not justify emotional abuse either. In addition, Mr Bennet shows a similar lack of empathy towards even the most loving, calm and amiable of his daughters. In his comments to Elizabeth regarding Jane's heartache and disappointment over Mr Bingley he jokes:

> So Lizzy, your sister is crossed in love I find. I congratulate her. Next to being married, a girl likes to be crossed in love a little now and then. It is something to think of and gives her a sort of distinction among her companions. (pp.137–8)

Despite having lived in the same house with Jane for her entire 22 years of life, when he lumps her in with the generic category of immature girls, Mr Bennet shows that he is stunningly unaware of her fine character or her emotional depth as a woman.

Elizabeth's natural love for her father, coupled with her admiration for his intelligence and appreciation of his attentions to her, has blinded her to his failings. In childhood our own family, the centre of our young universe, is the norm to which all others are compared. This changes gradually but, in Elizabeth's case, has taken longer because she has had so few experiences outside the small social circle where her parents are both long-established and high-status members. However, when Colonel Fitzwilliam unintentionally discloses his cousin Darcy's influence in discouraging Bingley from furthering his relationship with Jane, her awareness of her family as seen through the eyes of the wider world receives an unsettling prod:

> To Jane herself...there could be no possibility of objection. All loveliness and goodness as she is!... Neither could any thing be urged against my father, who, though with some peculiarities, has abilities which Mr Darcy himself need not disdain, and respectability which he will probably never reach. (pp.186–7)

Elizabeth acknowledges 'peculiarities', but as minor eccentricities or quirks, not as significant concerns. Very soon, however, she is forced to look at the effects of these more seriously.

In Darcy's letter to her, following her rejection of his marriage proposal, he refers to 'that total want of propriety so frequently, so almost uniformly betrayed by [your mother], by your three younger sisters, and occasionally even by your father' (p.198). At last Elizabeth must painfully acknowledge 'the unhappy defects' (p.212) of her family, particularly as she recognizes the shocking inappropriateness of her father's behaviour as he, 'contented with laughing at them, would never exert himself to restrain the wild giddiness of his youngest daughters' (p.213).

When she returns to Longbourn and hears of Lydia's invitation to go to Brighton with the militia under the doubtful chaperonage of the young and recently married Mrs Forster, Elizabeth tries to bring her father to understand 'all the improprieties of Lydia's general behaviour' (p.230). Although she speaks in the strongest of terms her father is not able to respond to her evident emotion or to see the wider implications of Lydia's behaviour beyond how it inconveniences him. Once again he betrays the problem with *central coherence*, which is often displayed by those on the autistic spectrum when trying to understand complex emotional situations:

> 'If you were aware,' said Elizabeth, 'of the very great disadvantage to us all, which must arise from the public notice of Lydia's unguarded and imprudent manner; nay, which has already arisen from it, I am sure you would judge differently in the affair.'
>
> 'Already arisen!' repeated Mr Bennet, 'what, has she frightened away some of your lovers? Poor little Lizzy! But do not be cast down. Such squeamish youths as cannot bear to be connected with a little absurdity, are not worth a regret. Come, let me see the list of the pitiful fellows who have been kept aloof by Lydia's folly.' (p.231)

Attwood and other researchers have noted that '[o]ne of the features of Asperger's Syndrome…is a tendency to laugh or giggle in circumstances when one would anticipate an expression of embarrassment, discomfort, pain or sadness' (1998, p.159). Despite his daughter's evident distress Mr Bennet is unable to match his emotions to hers. His jokes are jarringly inappropriate. In vain, Lizzy continues to try to help him see Lydia's and Kitty's behaviour from the perspective of their peers in society:

> Our importance, our respectability in the world, must be affected by the wild volatility, the assurance and disdain of all restraint which mark Lydia's character. Excuse me – for I must speak plainly. If you, my dear father, will not take the trouble of checking her exuberant spirits, and of teaching her…she will soon be beyond the reach of amendment. Her character will be fixed…and from the ignorance and emptiness of her mind, wholly unable to ward off any portion of the universal contempt which her rage for admiration will excite. In this danger Kitty is also comprehended. She will follow wherever Lydia leads. Vain, ignorant, idle, and absolutely uncontrolled! Oh! my dear father, can you suppose it possible that they will not be censured and despised wherever they are known, and that their sisters will not be often involved in the disgrace? (p.231)

To the passion and good sense of Elizabeth's pleading her father responds with affection and with a compliment about her and Jane. However, his focus remains on his own convenience as he cannot shift to perceive the situation from the point of view of his most beloved daughter or of society. As at the Netherfield ball he does not realize how he and his family appear to the rest of the world. He responds, 'We shall have no peace at Longbourn if

Lydia does not go to Brighton. Let her go then' (p.232). Then he offhand-edly drops his parental duties towards his youngest child on a man he has met only briefly as he says, 'Colonel Forster is a sensible man, and will keep her out of any real mischief' (p.232). At no time does he recall that Colonel Forster's actual responsibilities include an entire regiment, which might require a significant proportion of his time and thought.

Mr Bennet's inability to picture either Lydia's vulnerability in Brighton or the future of his family after his death are examples of the stunning lack of imagination of some on the autistic spectrum. Although Lizzy is vividly able to imagine the likely outcome of Lydia consorting further with the offi-cers, her father is not.

Elizabeth leaves her father 'disappointed and sorry' (p.232) that she had not been able to convince him of the validity of her concerns:

> Had Elizabeth's opinion been all drawn from her own family, she could not have formed a very pleasing picture of conjugal felicity or domestic comfort. Her father captivated by youth and beauty, and that appearance of good humour, which youth and beauty generally give, had married a woman whose weak understanding and illiberal mind, had early in their marriage put an end to all real affection for her. Respect, esteem, and confidence, had vanished for ever; and all his views of domestic happiness were overthrown... He was fond of the country and of books; and from these tastes had arisen his prin-cipal enjoyments. To his wife he was very little otherwise indebted, than as her ignorance and folly had contributed to his amusements. This is not the sort of happiness which a man would in general wish to owe to his wife; but where other powers of entertainment are wanting, the true philosopher will derive benefit from such as are given. (p.236)

The blame for the problems in the Bennet family is attributed by many largely to the 'ignorance and folly' of Mrs Bennet. However, it is no nobler to be amused by such traits than it is to possess them. If Mr Bennet had emo-tional as well as academic intelligence he would lead his family rather than merely laugh at them:

> Elizabeth, however, had never been blind to the impropriety of her father's behaviour as a husband. She had always seen it with pain; but respecting his abilities, and grateful for this affectionate treat-ment of herself, she endeavoured to forget what she could not overlook, and to banish from her thoughts that continual breach of

conjugal obligation and decorum which, in exposing his wife to the contempt of her own children, was so highly reprehensible. But she had never felt so strongly as now, *the disadvantages which must attend the children of so unsuitable a marriage*, nor ever been so fully aware of the evils arising from so ill-judged a direction of talents; talents which rightly used, might at least have preserved the respectability of his daughters, even if incapable of enlarging the mind of his wife. (p.236, my italics)

In the patriarchal society of the time, neglect by the father conveys a message of vulnerability to predators such as Wickham. As Elizabeth later acknowledges to her Aunt Gardiner:

Lydia has no brothers to step forward; and he might imagine, from my father's behaviour, from his indolence and the little attention he has ever seemed to give to what was going forward in his family, that *he* would do as little, and think as little about it as any father could do, in such a matter. (p.283)

It is not her mother's silliness alone that has put Lydia at risk; her father's self-centredness is equally to blame. For years he has been oblivious to the needs of his family and to the message that this gives to others.

Once Lydia runs away with Wickham, such a blatant breach of society's mores and morals jolts even such a self-focused, passive individual as Mr Bennet into recognizing the seriousness of the situation. The intense emotionality overwhelms him to the point that he is not able to process it immediately. Jane writes to Lizzy, 'I never saw him so affected' (p.275) and 'his excessive distress will not allow him to pursue any measure in the best and safest way' (p.276). Verbally she tells her sister, 'I never saw anyone so shocked. He could not speak a word for a full ten minutes' (p.292). Jane adds that he headed to London without communicating his plans to his distraught family, beyond his intention of trying to trace Lydia and Wickham by discovering the number of the hackney coach in which the pair had travelled. 'I do not know of any other designs that he had formed; but he was in such a hurry to be gone, and his spirits so greatly discomposed, that I had difficulty in finding out even so much as this' (p.293).

Once away Mr Bennet lacks the sensitivity to others or theory of mind to be aware of how desperately his wife and other daughters will be craving information both about Lydia's well-being and his own. As would be a definite risk in their society, Mrs Bennet fears that he will challenge Wickham to a duel and be killed. This would, of course, result in their family being instantly homeless as well as disgraced. However, Mr Bennet sends them no letters of reassurance or any other kind:

> The whole party were in hopes of a letter from Mr Bennet the next morning, but the post came in without bringing a single line from him. His family knew him to be on all common occasions, a most negligent and dilatory correspondent, but at such a time, they had hoped for exertion. They were forced to conclude, that he had no pleasing intelligence to send, but even of *that* they would have been glad to be certain. (p.294)

Mr Bennet has rarely considered his family's needs in the past and he does not yet again. In contrast to his lack of consideration, his brother-in-law, Mr Gardiner, is someone from whom the family 'were certain at least of receiving constant information of what was going on' (p.294). In his thoughtful and empathic way he understands that not knowing is often more stressful than even the worst information: 'Mr Gardiner left Longbourn on Sunday; on Tuesday, his wife received a letter from him' (p.295).

When Mr Bennet returns from London, he has 'all the appearance of his usual philosophic composure. He said as little as he had ever been in the habit of saying; made no mention of the business that had taken him away, and it was some time before his daughters had courage to speak of it' (p.299). Once again, as is typical of many on the spectrum, he shows a limited range of emotions; his 'philosophic composure' could also be described in the psychological terms of our day as limited facial affect. He continues to be staggeringly oblivious to his family's intense desire for any information he can provide.

When he does start to talk with Elizabeth he shows some fledgling awareness of how his failings as a father have contributed to their family's disgrace. When she starts to comfort him, he says, 'No, Lizzy, let me once in my life feel how much I have been to blame' (p.299). He also shows a temporary flash of insight into his nature when he adds, 'I am not afraid of being overpowered by the impression. It will pass away soon enough' (p.299).

This observation of his matches that of modern researchers in the field of autistic spectrum disorders as they have noted that there is 'a problem of initiation and generalisation. That is, the person knows what to do but cannot make the first move or does not recognise the cues that indicate that the skills can be used in different situations' (Attwood 1998, p.44). Literally within minutes after saying that he knows that he must shoulder some blame for Lydia's failings, Mr Bennet is teasing and tormenting Kitty as insensitively as always. He tells her that, in order to prevent her from running away like Lydia, many sanctions will be imposed including the dire consequence that 'balls will be absolutely prohibited, unless you stand up with one of your sisters' (p.300). When Kitty, overwrought and also unable to work out her father's character, 'took all these threats in a serious light' (p.300) and is reduced to tears, he continues to tease and bewilder her. Although earlier in the same interaction he says, 'I have at last learnt to be cautious' (p.300), he blatantly demonstrates that he has learnt nothing at all about the need to treat his young daughters with care and respect.

As could be predicted, shortly thereafter, once the marriage arrangements for Lydia are complete, Mr Bennet 'naturally returned to all his former indolence' (p.309), making no effort to become more involved in the academic or moral educations of either Mary or Kitty, who are still of an age to benefit. He is not able to generalize from the one experience to recognize that his errors with Lydia might also apply to his other daughters, particularly Kitty who had been so under her influence.

Although Mr Bennet has briefly been aware of some of his weaknesses, he remains unable to process emotional information quickly and continues to be oblivious to the natural and intense desire of the others to know anything that pertains to the youngest member of their family. When an extremely important letter comes from Mr Gardiner he shares it with no one, not even Lydia's mother, but walks into the woods in some mental confusion:

> 'Dear madam,' cried Mrs Hill, in great astonishment, 'don't you know there is an express come for master from Mr Gardiner? He has been here this half hour, and master has a letter.'
>
> Away ran the girls...through the vestibule into the breakfast room; from thence to the library; – their father was in neither...[they] ran across the lawn after their father, who was deliberately pursuing his way towards a small wood on one side of the paddock.
>
> ...[Elizabeth] eagerly cried out, 'Oh, Papa, what news? what news? have you heard from my uncle?'...
>
> ... 'Read it aloud,' said their father, 'for I hardly know myself what it is about.' (pp.301–2)

Finally the letter is shared, announcing that Lydia has been found and that her marriage to Wickham can be arranged. To do so Mr Gardiner requires that his brother-in-law send him 'full powers to act in your name...as soon as you can' (p.303):

> 'And have you answered the letter?' said Elizabeth.
> 'No; but it must be done soon.'
> 'Oh! my dear father,' she cried, 'come back, and write immediately. Consider how important every moment is, in such a case.' (p.303)

Mr Bennet is convinced by his daughters to overcome his inertia and dislike of the task, and to return to the house to start writing:

> It now occurred to the girls that their mother was in all likelihood perfectly ignorant of what had happened. They went to the library, therefore, and asked their father, whether he would not wish them to make it known to her. He was writing, and, without raising his head, coolly replied, 'Just as you please.'
> 'May we take my uncle's letter to read to her?'
> 'Take whatever you like, and get away.' (p.305)

Once again Mr Bennet is unable to think beyond his own feelings to consider those of others. Although his wife's anxious concern for their youngest daughter has been loudly obvious to everyone else in their entire community, he makes no effort to allay it. Most people want to share good news as rapidly as possible, especially in cases where there has been realistic fear about the well-being of a missing person. In addition, the blunt 'get away' of Mr Bennet's last response is indicative of the difficulty many on the spectrum have shifting their attention from one thing to another even momentarily. They tend to have a very low tolerance for being interrupted.

As an eventful year circles back on itself, September returns and once again Mrs Bennet is trying to ensure that her husband rouses himself to contribute to their four remaining daughters' futures by renewing acquaintance with the still eligible Mr Bingley:

> The subject which had been so warmly canvassed between their parents, about a twelvemonth ago, was now brought forward again.
> 'As soon as ever Mr Bingley comes, my dear,' said Mrs Bennet, 'you will wait on him of course.'

'No, no. You forced me into visiting him last year, and promised if I went to see him, he should marry one of my daughters. But it ended in nothing, and I will not be sent on a fool's errand again.'

His wife represented to him how absolutely necessary such an attention would be from all the neighbouring gentlemen, on his returning to Netherfield.

'Tis an etiquette I despise,' said he. 'If he wants our society let him seek it. He knows where we live. I will not spend my hours in running after neighbours every time they go away and come back again.'

'Well, all I know is, that it will be abominably rude if you do not wait on *him*.' (p.332)

Yet again Mr Bennet makes one of his ambiguous remarks, which can be viewed either as witty or as profoundly revealing about his inability to understand some of the subtleties of communication. Many on the spectrum would think that a guarantee rather than an optimistic prediction had been made when Mrs Bennet said that Mr Bingley would fall in love with one of their girls. Even highly intelligent people on the autistic spectrum can be extremely literal and often complain that they wish people would say what they really mean.

When Mr Bingley permanently re-enters their lives and Mr Bennet goes shooting with his future son-in-law, we see how someone with excellent social skills can help an ASD individual function at his or her optimum level. 'There was nothing of presumption or folly in Bingley, that could provoke his [Mr Bennet's] ridicule, or disgust him into silence, and he was more communicative and less eccentric than the others had ever seen him' (p.346). This may contribute to why he is closest to his two most socially adept daughters; especially to Elizabeth since she combines strong social abilities with intelligence.

Therefore, after Lady Catherine's unexpected visit to their home, he actually emerges voluntarily from his library to seek out Lizzy in order to share with her a third letter from Mr Collins. He is amused to learn that his cousin suspects the possibility that Elizabeth will wed his patroness's nephew. He exclaims:

'Mr Darcy, who never looks at any woman but to see a blemish, and who probably never looked at you in his life! It is admirable!'

Elizabeth tried to join in her father's pleasantry, but could only force one most reluctant smile. Never had his wit been directed in a manner so little agreeable to her.

'Are you not diverted?'

'Oh! yes. Pray read on.'

'... But, Lizzy, you look as if you did not enjoy it. You are not going to be Missish, I hope, and pretend to be affronted at an idle report. For what do we live, but to make sport for our neighbours, and laugh at them in our turn?'

'Oh!' cried Elizabeth, 'I am excessively diverted. But it is so strange!'

'Yes – that is what makes it amusing... And pray, Lizzie, what said Lady Catherine about this report? Did she call to refuse her consent?'

To this question his daughter replied only with a laugh; and as it had been asked without the least suspicion, she was not distressed by his repeating it. Elizabeth had never been more at a loss to make her feelings appear what they were not. It was necessary to laugh, when she would rather have cried. Her father had most cruelly mortified her, by what he said of Mr Darcy's indifference, and she could do nothing but wonder at such a want of penetration, or fear that perhaps, instead of his seeing too little, she might have fancied too much. (pp.362–4)

Lizzy still values her father's knowledge and intelligence so her fragile confidence is shaken by his certainty that Darcy is indifferent to her. She does not realize that her father is one of the last people who would have noticed subtle signs of interest, such as how often Darcy watches her. Mr Bennet is in tune with his favourite daughter enough to notice that initially she does not seem to find the letter as enjoyable as he does, but he is easily taken in by her acting amused even though she trembles on the verge of tears. As Lizzy feared, his problem is indeed that once again he sees too little.

Also in this conversation with his daughter he shares his cynical definition of the purpose of life as being 'to make sport for our neighbours and to laugh at them in our turn' (p.364). As Halperin says in his article 'Inside *Pride and Prejudice*':

everything in the book up to this point asks us to read Mr Bennet's statement ironically – as the speech of a man who, by practising the kind of detachment he defines here, has ruined the life of one of his daughters and made possible one of the most ill-assorted and unpleasant marriages in English literature. The only real question is whether or not Mr Bennet is *speaking* ironically here – whether he is *aware* of the monstrous nature of the philosophy he articulates in the 'making sport of our neighbours' speech... Mr Bennet has now experienced at firsthand the perils of detachment; surely he has no further desire to make sport of his neighbours. (1989, p.42)

Unfortunately, given that Mr Bennet shows so many indications of being on the autistic spectrum, he will not have been able to generalize from his own family's situation to the broader picture. As an individual with autism, his empathy for others is limited. Therefore, in answer to John Halperin's question, it is my opinion that Mr Bennet is not being deliberately ironic. Sadly, he is expressing his true perspective. If even his wife and dependent children are sources of amusement and often not treated with basic human decency, then there is little hope for others less closely connected to him. He makes fun of his neighbours because he cannot empathize with them or imagine that they can experience a rich array of feelings. In her article, 'Laughing at our neighbours: Jane Austen and the problem of charity', Sarah Emsley says, 'it is not enough to laugh at our neighbors and retreat from the world. The full practice of the theological virtue of charity demands engagement with the social world' (2006, p.9). Such engagement is exactly what has always been so difficult for Mr Bennet and for others who fall near him on the autistic spectrum.

The fact that, as he himself predicted, any sense of his own failings has 'passed away soon enough' (p.299) is demonstrated in his conversation with Lizzy after Darcy has asked him for her hand in marriage. Although he is expressing some true concern for her future happiness, his comments indicate that he still feels that he is the one who has suffered rather than caused suffering in his own marriage: 'Your lively talents would place you in the greatest danger in an unequal marriage... My child, let me not have the grief of seeing *you* unable to respect your partner in life. You know not what you are about' (p.376). Although he has briefly been able to be concerned for someone else, as the conversation continues, he slides back into being self-focused. When Lizzy tells him, 'what Mr Darcy had voluntarily done for Lydia... [h]e heard her with astonishment' and then exclaimed, 'So much the better. It will save me a world of trouble and economy' (p.377).

Given that taking *any* let alone '*a world* of trouble' over his family's well-being is not something he does or is able to do often, fortunately the vulnerable Kitty is removed from his household to spend 'the chief of her time with her two elder sisters. In society so superior to what she had generally known, her improvement was great' (p.385). We hear that with his family circle reduced to his wife and middle daughter, 'Mr Bennet missed his second daughter exceedingly; his affection for her drew him oftener from home than anything else could do. He delighted in going to Pemberley, especially when he was least expected' (p.385).

Yet again, Jane Austen has brilliantly noted and captured another sometimes maddening trait of some of those on the spectrum. Due to their difficulty thinking of the world from anyone else's perspective, they are exactly the people most likely to land on a friend or relative's doorstep when 'least expected' (p.385), without giving any prior warning let alone checking to see if it is convenient. However, this is merely a minor and irritating annoyance compared to Mr Bennet's more serious flaws.

Given the genuine dangers of such a self-centred person having responsibility for the care and teaching of children, it is perhaps fortunate that many as severely impaired as Mr Bennet marry late in life or not at all, hence rarely become parents. Some do, however. Tragically others besides Lydia have been victims of sexual predators due to their ASD parents' naïvety and their inability to read the subtle clues of changes in their child's behaviour. Neither is Kitty alone in having had her feelings trodden on repeatedly. Sadly, many others besides Jane and Lizzy have been mortified to the depths of their being and lived constantly on the alert to try to keep their parents' behaviour within socially acceptable limits. As Elizabeth recognizes so painfully and strongly, there are enormous 'disadvantages which must attend the children of so unsuitable a marriage' (p.236).

8

Mrs Bennet

'with manners so far from right herself' (p.213)

While Mr Bennet is introduced to us as being 'so odd a mixture' (p.5) that his character is hard to understand, Jane Austen seems much more certain about Mrs Bennet. Rather crisply as the book begins she tells us that:

> *Her* mind was less difficult to develope. She was a woman of mean understanding, little information, and uncertain temper. When she was discontented she fancied herself nervous. The business of her life was to get her daughters married; its solace was visiting and news. (p.5)

Ironically, on the preceding pages (pp.3,4), Mrs Bennet has actually shown far more common sense and better understanding than has her life partner. She may be a woman of 'little information' in the factual/academic definition but her emotional and social intelligence is slightly more developed than her spouse's. Unlike him, as noted earlier, she has instantly grasped the potentially life-changing significance for their daughters of the arrival of an eligible bachelor in their neighbourhood. If the 'business of her life' is to find partners and security for her daughters is that not showing more concern for them than does their father, whose business of life is to barricade himself in with his books? As she has no doubt had to do at other times in their 22 years of parenting she urges her husband to 'consider your daughters' (p.4). She defends them while trying to make him see the callousness of his criticisms that they are 'silly and ignorant' (p.5). We should be joining her when she asks, 'Mr Bennet, how can you abuse your own children in such a way?' (p.5). She rightly names it as abuse. Verbal abuse and neglect are both serious forms of child abuse, with consequences that can be as damaging as the more obvious physical forms.

Mrs Bennet then confronts him with his long-standing emotional abuse and insensitivity to herself as she cries out, 'You take delight in vexing me. You have no compassion on my poor nerves' (p.5). Again, this woman, whom we have been encouraged to look down upon, is correct. Her husband does tease her cruelly and never shows her compassion or empathy. In another of his responses, which can be viewed as amusing from one angle but shockingly insensitive from another, he responds sarcastically:

> You mistake me, my dear. I have a high respect for your nerves. They are my old friends. I have heard you mention them with consideration these twenty years at least. (p.5)

Yes, *she* has mentioned them, but when has *he* ever truly considered them?

Throughout the novel we see how Mr Bennet unthinkingly jokes about his wife's loss of her home if he predeceases her, how he holds her up to ridicule in front of their children and how he does not respond to her pleas for emotional support. These are all things that increase rather than decrease her 'nerves', which we might now refer to as severe anxiety or depression. In her response to him Mrs Bennet can only say, 'Ah! you do not know what I suffer' (p.5). And again she is stating the truth. He does not. As a man on the autistic spectrum he has a very limited to non-existent ability to see situations from her point of view or to 'put himself in her shoes'. As we have realized he cannot even relate to something as tangible as physical homelessness let alone more subtle emotional needs.

'Depression can be a normal reaction to having a partner with Asperger Syndrome' (2000, p.47), stated Attwood in his workshop for partners of people with autistic spectrum disorders. A participant is quoted as saying that often someone with a partner on the spectrum 'lives on the edge of a nervous breakdown' (2000, p.46). Aston, in her research, found that:

> All the neuro-typical women in the relationships stated that their mental and sometimes physical health had suffered as a consequence of being in a relationship with an autistic spectrum man. Many of the neuro-typical women were on or had been on anti-depressants; they reported feeling exhausted, frustrated, desperate and lonely and many thought they were going mad. (2003, p.166)

Mr Bennet offers in response to his wife's symptoms only 'I hope you will get over it' (p.5).

. Unfortunately for her, Mrs Bennet was chosen as a bride by a man likely to cause an increase in her negative qualities and then blame her for them. If married to a caring man, who both treated her with affection and filled the expected role of providing financial security for her and their children, she would have felt calmer and therefore less prone to her overwhelming anxiety attacks. 'When anxious the person increases their expression of Asperger's Syndrome, yet when happy and relaxed one may have to be very skilled to recognize the signs' (Attwood 1998, p.154). Although Mrs Bennet shows some autistic spectrum traits, particularly difficulty with both voice modulation and empathy, as well as a tendency to focus on minor details, these are comparatively mild. She does enjoy and seek out the company of others, and has some, albeit fluctuating, insight into social behaviour. If assured of financial stability for her old age and guided by a kind, loving partner, her more positive traits would have been brought to the forefront rather than her least attractive ones.

Very early in the book, while paying a call at Netherfield, she firmly states, 'What an agreeable man Sir William is...so genteel and easy! – He has always something to say to everybody. – That is my idea of good breeding' (p.44). Again Sir William is someone whose emotional intelligence has sometimes been discounted, while his lack of intellectual interests and wit have been emphasized. Mrs Bennet, to some degree, recognizes that Sir William is a person whom we would now call a 'connector' in that he facilitates positive social interactions between others. A marked contrast to Mr Bennet, he would have made Mrs Bennet a far better husband. He is initially described as a man who, recently elevated to knighthood and now retired from trade, is content to:

> occupy himself solely in being civil to all the world. For though elated by his rank, it did not render him supercilious; on the contrary, he was all attention to everybody. By nature inoffensive, friendly and obliging, his presentation at St James's had made him courteous. (p.18)

Courteous, civil, obliging, inoffensive; truly a man who treats all well and who does unto others as he would have them do unto him. Mrs Bennet shows some degree of sense when she values Sir William's inclusive social skills.

However, there are enough times when she does not show such good sense that her mild autistic traits are revealed. With her focus firmly fixed on marriage for her daughters, Mrs Bennet does not always recall the bigger picture, such as the fact that they need to be kept alive to be wed. Her intellect is sufficient for her to think out a scheme that will throw Jane into Mr Bingley's company when she is rain-stayed overnight at Netherfield. Although her sisters feel uneasy about Jane's safety on the journey, her mother proudly congratulates herself on the unexpected additional success of her idea when Jane develops an illness that necessitates a multiple-day visit. So pleased is she with what she has contrived that she does not see the situation from Jane's perspective at all. When she comes to Netherfield to check on the invalid, Austen states that '[h]ad she found Jane in any apparent danger, Mrs Bennet would have been very miserable' (p.41), revealing that she is a caring enough mother to be somewhat tuned into Jane's physical well-being. However, she cannot relate to her daughter's more subtle emotional needs so does not recognize that the entire subterfuge has been very humiliating for Jane and also for Elizabeth, as they feel all the awkwardness inherent in being uninvited house guests.

In her conversation with the Bingleys Mrs Bennet further reveals that she takes words literally, without reading the non-verbal messages of tone of voice and facial expression. Although Miss Bingley's offer to have Miss Bennet remain is made 'with cold civility' (p.10), Mrs Bennet is 'profuse in her acknowledgements' and refers to them as 'such good friends' (p.42).

Ironically, given how she later ignores Lizzy's attempts to prevent her from doing exactly that, she urges her second daughter to 'remember where you are, and do not run on in the wild manner that you are suffered to do at home' (p.42) when she feels that she is speaking in too bold a manner to Mr Bingley about how perfectly she understands his character. She feels that this disliked daughter is bordering on being discourteous, yet only moments later escalates a casual comment from Mr Darcy into an overly spirited defence of country life. She is unable to modulate the tone of her retort so sounds very rude, causing everyone else attending to the conversation to either blush, if they are related to her, or give 'expressive smiles' (p.43) if they are not.

As she gathers her younger daughters to depart, Mrs Bennet once again demonstrates that she takes in only the verbal rather than the non-verbal messages directed at her. She:

> began repeating her thanks to Mr Bingley for his kindness to Jane, with an apology for troubling him also with Lizzy. Mr Bingley was unaffectedly civil in his answer and forced his younger sister to be civil also, and say what the occasion required. She performed her

part indeed without much graciousness, but Mrs Bennet was satisfied. (p.45)

Other conversations reinforce our impression of Mrs Bennet as someone who is not able to discern subtle undercurrents or mixed messages. When Mr Collins is 'eloquent in [the] praise' of Lady Catherine he gives many examples that more discerning persons than either he or Mrs Bennet would recognize as betraying how officious and rude the ruler of Rosings actually is. He proudly describes how she 'had sent for him only the Saturday before, to make up her pool of quadrille in the evening', and how she:

> had even condescended to advise him to marry as soon as he could, provided he chose with discretion; and had once paid him a visit in his humble parsonage; where she had perfectly approved all the alterations he had been making, and had even vouchsafed to suggest some herself, – some shelves in the closets up stairs. (p.66)

To this list of interference and lack of consideration Mrs Bennet replies naïvely, 'That is all very proper and civil, I am sure…and I dare say she is a very agreeable woman' (p.67).

At the Netherfield ball, Mrs Bennet is far from proper herself but rather loud and indiscreet despite Lizzy's attempts to help her understand the negative impression her words are creating. Like her youngest daughter she has difficulty modulating her voice, so her remarks can be heard by the entire room rather than only by her conversational partner. Once set on a course of action/conversation she has trouble shifting:

> deeply was she [Lizzy] vexed to find that her mother was talking…freely, openly, and of nothing else but of her expectation that Jane would be soon married to Mr Bingley. – It was an animating subject, and Mrs Bennet seemed incapable of fatigue while enumerating the advantages of the match…
>
> In vain did Elizabeth endeavour to check the rapidity of her mother's words, or persuade her to describe her felicity in a less audible whisper; for to her inexpressible vexation, she could perceive that the chief of it was overheard by Mr Darcy, who sat opposite to them. Her mother only scolded her for being nonsensical.
>
> 'What is Mr Darcy to me, pray, that I should be afraid of him? I am sure we owe him no such particular civility as to be obliged to say nothing he may not like to hear.'

'For heaven's sake, madam, speak lower. – what advantage can it be to you to offend Mr Darcy? – You will never recommend yourself to his friend by so doing.'

Nothing that she would say, however, had any influence. Her mother would talk of her views in the same intelligible tone. Elizabeth blushed and blushed again with shame and vexation. (pp.99–100)

Poor Elizabeth has reason to blush yet again as next Mary draws negative attention to their family by singing poorly, and then Mr Collins delivers his monologue on the profession of a clergyman so loudly that it is heard by half the room. The majority react with stares and smiles, but Mrs Bennet is oblivious to these and to the inappropriateness of his speech as she 'seriously commended Mr Collins for having spoken so sensibly, and observed in a half-whisper to Lady Lucas, that he was a remarkably clever, good kind of young man, (p.101).

Mrs Bennet leaves the ball 'under the delightful persuasion' (p.103) that within months she will see her two eldest daughters suitably wed. However, the very next day both of her dreams are destroyed when Elizabeth rejects Mr Collins and Bingley leaves for London. Mrs Bennet reacts with anger towards Lizzy, with 'sour looks and ill-natured remarks' (p.127) towards Lady Lucas, whose daughter has been unexpectedly successful in the husband hunt, and towards Jane with a ceaseless monologue about Bingley's continued absence. Elizabeth and Jane avoid alluding to this last subject but:

no such delicacy restrained her mother, an hour seldom passed in which she did not talk of Bingley, express her impatience for his arrival, or even require Jane to confess that if he did not come back, she should think herself very ill used. (p.129)

These tirades worsen when 'Miss Bingley's letter arrived, and put an end to doubt' (p.133).

The emotional drain on poor, sweet Jane is so considerable that she cannot help saying, 'Oh! that my dear mother had more command over herself; she can have no idea of the pain she gives me by her continual reflections on him' (p.134). Sadly, this is true; she has 'no idea'. Mrs Bennet loves her eldest daughter, and admires her beauty and disposition. However, this love of her daughter's face is not sufficient to help her read it. She is not able to see the signs that her remarks are wounding her beloved firstborn.

Elizabeth's fears that her mother has damaged Jane's chances of marriage by her careless, gleeful talk in Mr Darcy's hearing are confirmed when she receives his letter following her rejection of his offer of marriage. As she reads it she has confirmation that, in the eyes of the polite world, her mother has 'manners so far from right' and was 'entirely insensible of the evil' (p.213) of the wild, giddy behaviour of her two youngest daughters. Insensible. Oblivious. Not noticing what others do. These words appear over and over again in the literature and research about those on the autistic spectrum.

The inevitable happens: Lydia disgraces the family. Mrs Bennet reacts:

> exactly as might be expected; with tears and lamentations of regret, invectives against the villainous conduct of Wickham, and complaints of her own sufferings and ill usage; blaming every body but the person to whose ill judging indulgence the errors of her daughter must be principally owing. (p.287)

The person or the pair? Ill-judgement has been shown but surely by both parents rather than merely one. Her ill-judgement was shown by indulgence but his, more passively, by neglect:

> 'If I had been able,' said she, 'to carry my point of going to Brighton, with all my family, this would not have happened; but poor dear Lydia had nobody to take care of her. Why did the Forsters ever let her go out of their sight? I am sure there was some great neglect or other on their side, for she is not the kind of girl to do such a thing, if she had been well looked after. I always thought they were very unfit to have the charge of her; but I was over-ruled, as I always am. Poor dear child!' (p.287)

Mrs Bennet is rewriting history as she had wanted to go to Brighton not so much to protect Lydia as to join in the socializing herself. Despite this motivation and her overall hysteria, her tirade contains a few kernels of truth. She does not blame Lydia but rather 'great neglect' (p.287) on the part of care givers. The neglect, however, was not the Forsters' but her family's. Lydia was doubly damned at birth by her neurological make-up and by having parents with similar weaknesses. For all that she has been joining in adult activities for some time, she is still a child mentally, emotionally and legally, even as her physical height and figure falsely proclaim maturity.

Already an anxious, unstable person, Mrs Bennet is overwhelmed by the repercussions of Lydia's behaviour. Regarding those with ASD who are

plagued by anxiety Attwood writes, '[f]or some, the level of anxiety fluctu-
ates and arrives in "waves" with periods of intense panic, followed by a
period of relative calm' (1998, p.154). In this case Lydia's escapade has triggered a tsunami of wild emotion. As Jane relates, 'My mother was taken ill
immediately, and the whole house in confusion!' and she further describes
her mother as 'in hysterics' (p.292). To her dear brother, Mrs Bennet cata-
logues her ills thus: 'I am frightened out of my wits; and have such
tremblings, such flutterings, all over me, such spasms in my side, and pains in
my head, and such beatings at heart, that I can get no rest by night nor by
day' (p.288). 'Hypochondria sometimes can be an expression of an anxiety
disorder,' according to Attwood (2000, p.5). However, despite her concerns
for her daughter, the underlying causes for this dreadful anxiety are still Mrs
Bennet's fear of homelessness if her husband dies, coupled with her knowledge that he has never taken her needs into account when deciding on his
actions. She begs Mr Gardiner, 'And, above all things, keep Mr Bennet from
fighting. Tell him what a dreadful state I am in' (p.288).

Attwood's observations about the calm following the storm prove to be
an accurate forecast in this case:

> As soon as Jane had read Mr Gardiner's hope of Lydia's being soon
> married, her [Mrs Bennet's] joy burst forth, and every following
> sentence added to its exuberance. She was now in an irritation as
> violent from delight, as she had ever been fidgetty from alarm and
> vexation... She was disturbed by no fear for her [Lydia's] felicity,
> nor humbled by any rememberance of her misconduct... 'How
> merry we shall be together when we meet!' (p.306)

Yet again Mrs Bennet shows herself to be oblivious to deeper emotions and
subtleties. If Lydia is married, she is married. It matters not how or to whom.
Mrs Bennet feels that she has achieved the first step towards her goal of matrimony for all her daughters so she expects everyone to rejoice with her:
'Many people with AS do not appear to experience feelings of embarrassment; this may be due to the inability to read other people's thoughts'
(Aston 2003, p.78). She has no awareness that others may be experiencing
different emotions or other concerns. She surges back into the mainstream
of life as she 'again took her seat at the head of her table, and in spirits
oppressively high. No sentiment of shame gave a damp to her triumph'
(p.310). Like Lydia, her attention is focused on a minor detail without the
ability to take in the big picture: 'She was more alive to the disgrace, which
the want of new clothes must reflect on her daughter's nuptials, than to any

sense of shame at her eloping and living with Wickham, a fortnight before they took place' (p.311).

When Lydia and her handsome husband pay their honeymoon visit to Longbourn:

> [h]er mother stepped forwards, embraced her, and welcomed her with rapture; gave her hand with an affectionate smile to Wickham, who followed his lady, and wished them both joy, with an alacrity which shewed no doubt of their happiness. (p.315)

Thus Mrs Bennet provides another excellent example of the difficulties with imagination experienced by some on the autistic spectrum. She is not able to project into the future to question whether this marriage bears any resemblance to the 'happily ever after' ending of fairy tales. Nor is she able to analyse the personalities of such a couple to see if they possess the attributes needed to handle the 'for better and for worse, for richer and for poorer' circumstances that life will bring them.

Given one daughter's 'success' Mrs Bennet is very encouraged when the news comes that Mr Bingley is returning to Netherfield. Once again she urges her husband to pay the expected formal welcoming visit to him and receives a similarly obtuse reply, which she correctly identifies as 'being abominably rude if you do not wait on him' (p.333). As always when she is focused on something, she lapses into endless monologues about it. Once again she does not notice how this affects her eldest daughter's spirits. Jane tells Lizzy:

> I could see him with perfect indifference, but I can hardly bear to hear it thus perpetually talked of. My mother means well; but she does not know, no one can know how much I suffer from what she says. (p.333)

Jane recognizes that her mother loves her and is concerned for her future so is fully aware that her mother's insensitivity to her feelings does not arise out of malice. However, Lizzy, with her highly developed emotional intelligence, can read the subtle indicators of Jane's emotions that their mother cannot. 'Elizabeth could easily perceive that her spirits were affected by it. They were more disturbed, more unequal, than she had often seen them' (p.332). The signs were there to be read, but Mrs Bennet is illiterate in that language.

When Bingley and Darcy unexpectedly come to visit on the third morning after their return to Hertfordshire, Mrs Bennet shows her underlying resemblance to Mr Collins in the style of her welcome. She does not hit quite the right note. Bingley 'was received by Mrs Bennet with a degree of civility, which made her two daughters ashamed' (p.335), and she maintains this tone throughout the visit:

> 'When you have killed all your own birds, Mr Bingley,' said [their] mother, 'I beg you come here, and shoot as many as you please, on Mr Bennet's manor. I am sure he will be vastly happy to oblige you, and will save all the best of the covies for you.' Elizabeth's misery increased, at such unnecessary, such officious attention! (p.337)

Again Mrs Bennet's manners are inappropriate when she is the hostess for a large shooting party and dinner at Longbourn. The etiquette of the day is followed in that at least one of the highest-status male guests is seated beside her; the other correctly recognizes and responds to the invitation in Jane's smile so joins her. Thus Elizabeth has to watch as Mr Darcy is seated on one side of her mother.

> She was not near enough to hear any of their discourse, but she could see how seldom they spoke to each other, and how formal and cold was their manner, whenever they did. Her mother's ungraciousness, made the sense of what they owed him more painful to Elizabeth's mind. (p.340)

To ignore a guest at your own table shows a shocking disregard for the comfort of another.

Unlike her father, when word came to him of Lydia's forthcoming wedding, Jane immediately wishes to relieve her mother's apprehensions by sharing the happy news of her betrothal: "'I must go instantly to my mother;" she cried. "I would not on any account trifle with her affectionate solicitude; or allow her to hear it from anyone but myself"' (p.347). Jane, an affectionate and kindhearted woman, shows much more awareness of her mother's love than did either Mr Bennet or Lydia with her offhand plan to relay news of her own marriage impersonally by letter as a 'good joke' (p.291).

When Lady Catherine De Bourgh descends in wrath upon Longbourn to inform Elizabeth that she must not consider marriage to her nephew, Darcy, she is so rude that she barely speaks to the woman she has impelled to be her hostess. However, Mrs Bennet once again betrays her lack of awareness of social subtleties when she feels honoured by the visit of a higher-ranking woman. She says contentedly that 'her calling here was pro-digiously civil' (p.359) when it was actually extraordinarily uncivil.

Ironically, one of the few times that Mrs Bennet does show sensitivity to a daughter's feelings, it is to express her sympathy for a situation that is actually very much to that daughter's secret wishes! Mrs Bennet's suggestion that a group of the young people walk to Oakham Mount is ultimately taken up by only two. In a consoling voice Mrs Bennet says:

> I am quite sorry, Lizzy, that you should be forced to have that dis-agreeable man all to yourself. But I hope you will not mind it: it is all for Jane's sake, you know; and there is no occasion for talking to him, except just now and then. So, do not put yourself to inconve-nience. (p.375)

Consistency of character is maintained, however, in that her advice recommends far from hospitable treatment to someone who is once again their guest. She may admire Sir William for being 'civil to all the world' (p.18) but she certainly does not practise that herself.

The black-and-white nature of her reactions to Bingley and Darcy are quite typical of the lack of subtlety in characterization shown by many with ASD. Her harsh opinions make it difficult for Elizabeth to approach her about her engagement as she:

> could not determine how her mother would take it; sometimes doubting whether all his wealth and grandeur would be enough to overcome her abhorrence of the man. But whether she was violently set against the match, or violently delighted with it, it was certain that her manner would be equally ill adapted to do credit to her sense; and she could no more bear that Mr Darcy should hear the first raptures of her joy, than the first vehemence of her disapproba-tion. (p.375)

A lifetime of experience has made Lizzy painfully aware of her mother's inability to regulate her emotions. To her great surprise, however, when she shares her news:

> Its effect was most extraordinary; for on first hearing it, Mrs Bennet sat quite still, and unable to utter a syllable. Nor was it under many, many minutes, that she could comprehend what she heard. (p.378)

When they hear something completely unexpected or highly emotional, many people on the autistic spectrum are not able to process it immediately.

Perhaps their difficulty with shifting focus means that they are unable to make room for such unexpected new information in their firmly set patterns of thought. Mrs Bennet does ultimately recover sufficiently to rejoice in as loud and inappropriate a manner as we would have predicted!

Following the double wedding of Mrs Bennet's two eldest daughters to two wealthy men, Jane Austen comments:

> I wish I could say, for the sake of her family, that the accomplish-
> ment of her earnest desire in the establishment of so many of her
> children, produced so happy an effect as to make her a sensible, ami-
> able, well-informed woman for the rest of her life; though perhaps it
> was lucky for her husband, who might not have relished domestic
> felicity in so unusual a form, that she still was occasionally nervous
> and invariably silly. (p.393)

The 'invariably silly' shows that her intellectual interests did not change, but the fact that she was only 'occasionally nervous' indicates that her behaviour was more stable when the very real fear of a homeless, impoverished old age was removed.

Mrs Bennet is a woman at the mild end of the autistic spectrum, whose symptoms are significantly aggravated by being married to a man who may be her superior intellectually but is her inferior in his ability to connect emotionally to others. Although they each feel sorry for themselves, it is their children who truly suffer. Following one of many unpleasant scenes, Elizabeth speaks for the feelings of all caught in the bewildering complexities of being normal children of autistic spectrum parents when she recognizes that 'years of happiness could not make...amends, for moments of such painful confusion' (p.337).

Poor Elizabeth

A cousin…two sisters…her father…her mother.

Empathetic readers over two centuries have felt deeply for Elizabeth as she copes with such an extremely puzzling and trying family.

At the ball at Netherfield we cringe with her as 'Elizabeth blushed and blushed again with shame and vexation. She could not help frequently glancing her eye at Mr Darcy, though every glance convinced her of what she dreaded' (p.100). '[It] had appeared, that had her family made an agreement to expose themselves as much as they could during the evening, it would have been impossible for them to play their parts with more spirit, or finer success…' (p.101)

However, at that point she had met none of *his* relations!

As among the Bennets, there are those in the Fitzwilliam connection whose behaviour provides ample cause for their more socially astute relatives to redden in discomfort.

Part Three

The Fitzwilliam Family

9

Anne De Bourgh

'spoke very little' (p.162)

Of all of the characters created by Jane Austen, Anne De Bourgh, Mr Darcy's maternal cousin, is the most blatantly autistic, showing traits from the severe, classic or Kanner's end of the spectrum rather than the milder or Asperger's end. However, we readers are understandably unaware of this, just as we tend to be unaware of her. We barely notice Anne at all as she rarely moves and we never hear her speak.

We initially hear mention of her in glowing terms as 'a most charming young lady' and 'far superior to the handsomest of her sex' (p.67), but this is truly a case where considering the source is essential. Mr Collins, echoing Lady Catherine, can hardly be considered an objective observer. Or a wise one. However, as he continues to tell his cousins of Miss Anne, he makes mention of 'a sickly constitution, which has prevented her from making that progress in many accomplishments which she could not otherwise have failed of' (p.67). Thus we are given our first clue that she has not acquired many of the skills considered basic for a young woman of her birth and wealth. A second clue follows when Mr Collins reveals that he has received this information from 'the lady who superintended her education, and still resides with them' (p.67). Although, in the terms of the day, this lady, Mrs Jenkinson, appears to have moved simply from the role of governess to that of lady's companion, in reality she actually functions more like a special education aide or life skills worker, 'scaffolding' her charge through a carefully structured day so that the veneer of normalcy is preserved.

The first glimpse that Maria Lucas and Elizabeth have of the heiress occurs when her carriage makes its daily stop outside the parsonage. With shock Maria describes her as 'thin and small', while Elizabeth adds the words 'sickly and cross' (p.158). Despite the trappings of fine garments and a fancy phaeton the person at the centre of this wealth is less than prepossessing in and of herself.

The adjectives thin, small and sickly are clues that Miss De Bourgh may be suffering from nutritional deficiencies possibly due to gastro-intestinal issues which have been noted to co-exist with autism in a sub-set of individuals. A recent article in Discover magazine (Niemark 2007) discusses research by Harvard pediatric neurologist, Martha Herbert, and others that in some cases autism is a neuroinflamatory disorder affecting the brain, the immune system and the gut. The adjective 'cross' tells us that her facial expression is far from appropriate for someone making a social call. However, it is her behaviour or lack thereof that excites even more comment than her appearance. Elizabeth instantly notes her lack of consideration for others and exclaims, 'She is abominably rude to keep Charlotte out of doors in all this wind. Why does she not come in?' Maria's explanation that 'Charlotte says she hardly ever does' (p.158) adds rigidity and strict adherence to routine to the characteristics of autism that Miss De Bourgh exhibits.

When the reader encounters Miss De Bourgh more closely at the first dinner party at Rosings, to the descriptors of 'pale and sickly' are added the detail that 'her features though not plain, were insignificant' (p.162). In other words she exhibited little facial expression — none of the vivaciousness and animation with which many share their emotions and reactions with others.

Based on her mother's later insistence to Elizabeth that Anne's engagement to her cousin Darcy was planned for them 'while in their cradles' (p.355), we can assume that she is in at least her mid- if not her late twenties. Generally a young woman living only in the company of two middle-aged ladies would welcome with alacrity the chance to associate with those closer to her in age. However, when such visitors come to Rosings, Anne has no direct interaction with either Elizabeth or Maria. During the preliminary conversations prior to the meal 'she spoke very little, except in a low voice to Mrs Jenkinson' (p.162). We are not made privy to those comments but they may well have been ones indicative of her lack of comfort in the situation, with its expectations of social interchange.

Anne is yet another who breaks the formal rule of spending equal time in conversation with those seated on either side at the dinner table as she 'said not a word to [Elizabeth] all dinner time' (p.163). Indeed she seems to have been extraordinarily passive as her companion on her other side, Mrs Jenkinson, 'was chiefly employed in watching how little Miss De Bourgh ate, pressing her to try some dish, and fearing that she was indisposed' (p.163). Again, digestive issues rather than social interaction seem to be dominating her meal. Also researchers have noted that 'some young adolescents with AS...may develop almost catatonic features' (Gilberg 1998). According to Wing and Shah (2000) catatonia is a term referring to a cluster of behaviours when they occur in 'sufficient degree to interfere with movement and everyday functions of self-care, education, occupation and leisure. The essential features are:

(a)   increased slowness affecting movements and verbal responses;

(b)   difficulty in initiating and completing actions;

(c)   increased reliance on physical or verbal prompting by others; and

(d)   increased passivity and apparent lack of motivation' (p.357).

Certainly Miss De Bourgh's almost complete lack of animation in a setting that should have been an enjoyable one for her indicates her minimal interest in or awareness of her surroundings.

This apparent inertia or passiveness is clearly described in Dr George T. Lynn's article, 'Five survival strategies to help children with Asperger's syndrome overcome inertia'. Dr Lynn explains:

> This lack of ability to initiate activity probably relates to the fact that Asperger's kids may be deeply apraxic when it comes to affective, cognitive, and behavioural tasks. That is, they do not automatically visualize what movements look like, what conversation with others might sound like, or generally what will happen in the future. Having no way of seeing the potential future, the child cannot plan his present action and so does nothing. (1999, p.1)

Anne's interest is finally aroused not by people but by numbers. Following the meal, 'Miss De Bourgh chose to play at casino... Their table was superlatively stupid. Scarcely a syllable was uttered that did not relate to the game' (p.166). Several years ago I observed a similar situation when an academically capable but socially awkward girl said barely a word during several hours of card games until she suddenly pointed out an esoteric mathematical pattern in the scores. She neither made eye contact with nor spoke to anyone else around the table except once to her older sister. The other young people present treated the game not as a mathematical equation but precisely as what it was – a game, hence a pleasant opportunity to laugh, joke and become better acquainted personally. It is likely that that young lady and Anne De Bourgh would agree with Lou Arrendale, a fictional man with autism in Elizabeth Moon's *The Speed of Dark*, who said about himself: 'Who I was thought abstract patterns of numbers were more important than abstract patterns of relationship' (2002, p.168).

Perhaps fortunately for the flow of the narrative, since she is far from being an engaging character, Miss De Bourgh makes only a few more appearances in the novel. Austen writes, 'how often especially Miss De Bourgh drove by in her phaeton... She not infrequently stopped at the Parsonage, and had a few minutes' conversation with Charlotte, but was scarcely ever prevailed on to get out' (p.168). Many on the autistic spectrum have 'a propensity to establish and enforce routines...once a pattern has emerged it must be maintained' (Attwood 1998, pp.91–2). Also, given that carriage riding is an essentially passive activity, one wonders if Miss De Bourgh's participation in the few minutes' conversation was as well. No doubt the interactions consisted of many repetitive comments about the weather and formal enquiries of the 'How are you today?' nature. One also wonders whether Miss Anne even produced this scripted, predictable conversation or whether she was merely an understudy while Mrs Jenkinson and Charlotte actually spoke for her in the same way that we all do for babies and pets. Is it truly a conversation when you both ask and answer your own questions?

When last we encounter Anne, as Elizabeth and Maria are taking their leave, 'Miss De Bourgh exerted herself so far as to curtsey and hold out her hand to both' (p.214). Neither gesture is spontaneous but rather a routine or script that could and would have been taught, indeed trained, very carefully.

Some may wonder if Miss Anne's quietness is due to being dominated by her mother, who certainly rarely leaves any gaps in a conversation for another to fill. However, Lady Catherine is not portrayed as unkind or bullying towards her daughter, and Anne's behaviour is the same whether or not her mother is present.

In summary, Miss Anne De Bourgh is extremely passive and withdrawn, with limited facial affect or ability to initiate conversation. She shows interest only when numbers are involved. One essayist expresses concern for her and asks:

> What is to become of Anne De Bourgh? I cannot judge it likely that she would marry a future duke or be allowed to marry a fortune-hunter, but if she outlives Lady Catherine she is going to be a sore

> trial to her cousins. She has never had to make a decision in her life
> and is probably incapable of doing so. (Glancy 1989, p.116)

Since her mother's plan that she be married off to her cousin, Darcy, has been thwarted, what will her future hold? In the short term, no doubt a relatively unchanging existence since there is the wealth to employ maids and companions to dress her and move her through the routines of the day. These routines, prompts and supports could continue whether or not a husband is actually found for her by her mother. We can only hope that Lady Catherine's groom-grasping eyes do not light on yet another cousin on the Fitzwilliam side of the family; the attractive Colonel deserves someone who could truly appreciate his sociability and kindness!

As to whether it would be possible to have a marriage involving someone with such strong autistic traits as Anne, the answer has certainly been 'yes' when either sufficient money or a title have been involved. The British tradition of eccentricity among its nobility may partly rest on exactly that sort of marriage if the histories of some noble families are taken as exemplars.

In his autobiography, *A Silver-plated Spoon*, John Russell, the 13th Duke of Bedford writes that his grandfather, the 11th Duke, had a 'curious habit of always looking down when he talked and a disconcerting way of deadening every conversational gambit' (1959, p.15). When he did speak it was usually to impart his extensive knowledge of animals and trees 'in a manner completely and utterly dead, like an encyclopaedia' (p.22). The 13th Duke states that his grandfather lived a 'completely lonely and austere life' in which 'everything went by the clock' (p.19). His life was so inflexibly regimented that 'his first course was always a cup of beef *consomme*. It was made exactly the same way every day, using precisely nine and a half pounds of the best shin of beef' (p.20). He met his almost equally distinctive, lower-ranking wife while serving with the Grenadier Guards in India. She was an academically orientated young woman, or 'bluestocking', who preferred to 'retire at frequent intervals to the top of the steeple in her father's church' (p.24) rather than participate in the usual social round. Similarly, their only child, the 12th Duke, is portrayed as 'very shy, very cold, very reserved with practically no friends' (p.36), and as having been 'a sensitive and nervous child, unable to acquire skill in many of the pursuits in which [his parents] would have liked him to excel' (p.34). Therefore, the 13th Duke muses, 'how my father ever brought himself to propose I cannot imagine' (p.36). His chosen bride, or target, was the daughter of one of his professors at Oxford so significantly beneath him both in rank and socio-economic class. Bedford records:

> My mother once told me that she used to pray that he would pro-pose to her sister rather than herself, but her mother, who was a terrible old snob and was enchanted with the idea of becoming con-nected with the dukedom of Bedford, pushed her into the marriage. (1959, p.36)

In reverse fashion some younger son or nephew of an impoverished noble family may be convinced by his mother and hers to offer for Miss Anne. Doubtless someone will value Rosings and its wealth enough to go through the motions of marrying her. Her purse, not her personality, may attract a partner.

10

Lady Catherine De Bourgh

'not rendered formidable by silence' (p.162)

If the daughter has little to say, the mother is her opposite. For once George Wickham speaks the truth when he says of Darcy's aunt, Lady Catherine De Bourgh, that 'her manners are dictatorial and insolent' (p.84), and makes reference to 'her authoritative manner' (p.84). Before we meet her we also hear from another with a much more positive view but, ironically, his anecdotes give us a similar image of a woman who directs others with little regard for their feelings. Mr Collins is honoured that 'she condescended to give…her opinion (unasked too)' on the subject of his marriage. He does not notice that her thoughts are centred around her comfort, not his, when she informs him that, 'A clergyman like you must marry,' and orders him to 'Chuse properly, chuse a gentlewoman for *my* sake' (p.105, original italics).

When Lizzy first meets Lady Catherine she sees 'a tall, large woman, with strongly-marked features, which might once have been handsome', so she discerns 'some resemblance of Mr Darcy'(p.162). This resemblance is not merely in countenance but also in deportment, as 'her air was not conciliating, nor was her manner of receiving them, such as to make her visitors forget their inferior rank' (p.162). However, she differed from her nephew in that '[she] was not rendered formidable by silence; but whatever she said was spoken in so authoritative a tone, as marked her self-importance' (p.162).

As the evening progresses Lady Catherine's focus on herself and lack of awareness of subtlety is evidenced in her pleased response to the thickly spread flattery provided by two of her guests, as 'every dish was commended, first by him [Mr Collins], and then by Sir William…in a manner which Elizabeth wondered Lady Catherine could bear. But Lady Catherine seemed gratified by their excessive admiration' (p.163). Otherwise, very little else is said as 'the party did not supply much conversation' (p.163).

Nor was the reciprocal flow of conversation in evidence as the evening progressed:

> When the ladies returned to the drawing room, there was little to be done but to hear Lady Catherine talk, which she did without any intermissions till coffee came in, delivering her opinion on every subject in so decisive a manner as proved that she was not used to having her judgement controverted. She enquired into Charlotte's domestic concerns familiarly and minutely, and gave her a great deal of advice. (p.163)

In between bestowing largesse from her overflowing cornucopia of counsel to Charlotte, 'she addressed a variety of questions to Maria and Elizabeth...[who] felt all the impertinence of her questions' (p.163). After asking after things that truly should have been no concern of hers, Lady Catherine then responds bluntly 'very strange' (p.164) and 'very odd' (p.165) when she does not approve of the responses. Although unaware of the impropriety of her own questions, ironically she believes she can identify it in the answers of others, chiding Elizabeth, 'you give your opinion very decidedly' (p.166).

When the party divides into two groups to play cards, Lady Catherine's table is, on the surface, the opposite of her daughter's silent one; however, at neither does true conversation flourish: 'Lady Catherine was generally speaking – stating the mistakes of the three others, or relating some anecdote of herself' (p.166). The evening does not draw to a close by mutual agreement but rather '[w]hen Lady Catherine and her daughter had played as long as *they* chose, the tables were broken up' (p.166; this time the italics are mine).

Throughout the evening Lady Catherine exhibits the impaired communication style typical of many autistic people in that she resorts to what researchers describe as 'incessant questioning and one-sided conversations' (Attwood 1998, p.20). Her remarks 'lack social and emotional reciprocity...[but] dominate the interaction' (p.29). As we have observed, she is also quite comfortable appointing herself as the arbitrator of the behaviour of others in her social circles and beyond. Gradually Elizabeth realizes that:

> though this great lady was not in the commission of the peace for the county, she was a most active magistrate in her own parish, the

minutest concerns of which were carried to her by Mr Collins: and whenever any of the cottagers were disposed to be quarrelsome, discontented or too poor, she sallied forth into the village to settle their differences, silence their complaints, and scold them into harmony and plenty. (p.169)

Ironically her self-centredness and lack of awareness of the feelings of others are most obvious when she congratulates herself on the depth of her emotions. After her nephews have embarked on their homeward journey she states with her usual certainty, 'I believe nobody feels the loss of friends so much as I do...[I] know them to be so much attached to me' (p.210).

When we next have the pleasure of Lady Catherine's company, her manners, fuelled by anger, are even less appropriate. She bursts into the Bennets' lives when it 'was too early in the morning for visitors' (p.351), thus showing no regard for the social mores of her society. 'She entered the room with an air more than usually ungracious, made no other reply to Elizabeth's salutation than a slight inclination of the head, and sat down without saying a word' (p.351). When she does initiate speech, it is done very rudely indeed referring to the lady of the house in the third person as 'That lady' (p.351) and then, dropping the noun, stating even less politely 'And *that* I suppose is one of your sisters' (p.352). When Mrs Bennet valiantly tries to maintain the semblance of a normal social call by using this opening to talk about her eldest daughter's marital prospects, Lady Catherine further exhibits her autistic tendencies by a very abrupt topic change: '"You have a very small park here," returned Lady Catherine after a short silence' (p.352). Additional topics and social niceties are attempted by the Bennet ladies with no success: 'Mrs Bennet, with great civility, begged her ladyship to take some refreshment; but, Lady Catherine very resolutely and not very politely, declined eating any thing' (p.352).

Lady Catherine does manage to request rather than command Elizabeth's company on a walk through the garden to the wilderness area, but 'they proceeded in silence along the gravel walk that led to the copse: Elizabeth was determined to make no effort for conversation with a woman, who was now more than usually insolent and disagreeable' (p.353). Once Lady Catherine does begin to talk again, her limited *theory of mind*, or ability to realize that others have different perspectives and knowledge, is very apparent:

> 'You can be at no loss, Miss Bennet, to understand the reason of my
> journey hither. Your own heart, your own conscience, must tell you
> why I come.'
>
> Elizabeth looked with unaffected astonishment.
>
> 'Indeed, you are mistaken, Madam. I have not been at all able to
> account for the honour of seeing you here.' (p.353)

In this scene with Elizabeth many of Lady Catherine's statements begin
with an emphatic 'I', which clearly indicates who she thinks is most affected
by the various marital possibilities under discussion:

> *I* insist on being satisfied.
>
> *I* am almost the nearest relation he has in the world, and am
> entitled to know all of his dearest concerns.
>
> *I* have not been used to submit to any person's whims. *I* have
> not been in the habit of brooking disappointment.
>
> *I* will not be interrupted. Hear me in silence.
>
> *I* am most seriously displeased. (pp.354–8, my italics)

Once she does indeed have to 'brook disappointment', Lady Catherine has
no idea how to lose gracefully nor does she realize that criticizing someone's beloved will not endear her to him. Once she hears that Darcy and
Elizabeth are to wed:

> Lady Catherine was extremely indignant on the marriage of her
> nephew; and as she gave way to all the genuine frankness of her
> character, in her reply to the letter which announced its arrange-
> ment, she sent him language so very abusive, especially of Elizabeth,
> that for some time all intercourse was at an end. (p.388)

In this novel Lady Catherine is the one character Jane Austen creates that
exhibits the difficulties controlling anger that can characterize a number of
those on the spectrum. As Aston writes:

> anger can present itself like a child's tantrum, it will erupt, cause a lot
> of stress to those around and then disappear. The AS person will
> often not be aware of the devastation and emotional pain their
> over-reaction has caused others. (2003, pp.87–8)

In this case the thwarted plans and frustration causing Lady Catherine's
anger are quite obvious but sometimes it can be 'very unpredictable and irra-
tional...appear[ing] completely out of context' (p.132). This is, of course,
particularly terrifying in a large man with small children or in anyone who

has power over others. We could speculate about various dictators of the past centuries...

Lady Catherine presents with many classic signs of autism in that she shows no awareness of the feelings or points of view of others. She is completely self-centred. Her verbal output consists almost exclusively of either monologues or interrogations. After these characteristics are made even more obvious during her uninvited visit to Longbourn, Lizzy rethinks her first impression of Lady Catherine as she asks herself: 'How could I ever think her like her nephew?' (p.353).

There is one paragraph in Dr Temple Grandin's book, *Thinking in Pictures* (1995) about the impact of autism on her life, which echoes what Jane Austen had one of her characters say in *Pride and Prejudice* in an achingly heartfelt moment of insight 200 years earlier.

> I have become more aware of a kind of electricity that goes on between people. I have observed that when several people are together and having a good time, their speech and laughter follow a **rhythm**. They will all laugh together and then talk quietly until the next laugh cycle. I have always had a hard time fitting in with this **rhythm**, and I usually interrupt conversations without realizing my mistake.
>
>   The problem is that I can't follow the **rhythm**. (Grandin, pp.91–2)
>
> *Thinking in Pictures,* 1995

> I certainly have not the talent which some people possess,' said Darcy, 'of conversing easily with those I have never seen before. I cannot catch their **tone** of conversation, or appear interested in their concerns, as I often see done. (Austen, p.175)
>
> *Pride and Prejudice,* 1795–1813

'Rhythm'...

...'tone'...

...not '**in tune**' with those around them...

11

Fitzwilliam Darcy

'I am ill qualified to recommend myself to strangers' (p.175)

For almost two centuries women have joined Elizabeth Bennet by falling in love with Mr Darcy, while academics have matched her struggles to try to understand his character.

In my opinion it is not pride but subtle autism that is the major reason for Darcy's frequent silences, awkward behaviour at social events and the monologue that he, like Mr Collins, delivers the first time he proposes to Elizabeth. Our recent and growing knowledge of the autistic spectrum is the crucial piece that has been needed to help solve the puzzle of his personality.

The key initiating event in the novel is Mr Darcy's behaviour the first time we, and Elizabeth, meet him. Everything else in this beloved book hinges on the poor 'First Impression' he makes. To his detriment, the initial encounter takes place in the sort of environment in which he is least able to appear at his best. A lively crowded scene filled with unfamiliar faces, noise, constant change, emotional undercurrents, flirtatious gestures and expressions; this is a description not of delight but of discomfort for many people on the spectrum. Mr Bennet avoided the entire affair; Darcy, with a more developed sense of duty, no doubt yielded to the united entreaties of the Bingley party to attend. The assembly ball at Meryton, which is so delightful an occasion for the majority of the local townsfolk, is not so for Mr Darcy or others like him. 'An atmosphere of intense socializing and noise is often not enjoyable for the [person] with Asperger's syndrome. At this time they are at their least skilled and most vulnerable' (Attwood 1998, p.39).

'Their least skilled and most vulnerable'. People don't necessarily have to look vulnerable on the outside to feel it on the inside. Although initially impressed by Darcy's build, looks and the reports of his wealth, the favourable opinion of the fine folk of Meryton soon falters as:

> his manners turned the tide of his popularity; for he was discovered to be proud, to be above his company, and above being pleased; and not all his large estate in Derbyshire could then save him from having a most forbidding disagreeable countenance, and being unworthy to be compared with his friend. (p.10)

The behaviour that makes the Merytonians change their minds about Mr Darcy consists of the facts that he:

> danced only once with Mrs Hurst and once with Miss Bingley, declined being introduced to any other lady, and spent the rest of the evening in walking about the room, speaking occasionally to one of his own party. (p.10)

If a short, homely tradesman named Mr Dobbey had behaved in this way he would probably not even have been noticed by anyone, let alone given offence. If some village worthies or a neglected spinster had paid this other Mr D any attention, they would have likely labelled his actions as due to shyness or lack of confidence. All that either Mr D has done is stick with the people he knows and walk about without joining any other group. Many, many ruder things have been done at parties!

However, Mr Darcy cannot blend into the corners of the room as can the multitude of Mr Dobbeys of the world. Due to Darcy's 'fine, tall person, handsome features, noble mien and...ten thousand a year' (p.10) others watch and comment on his every move. The same behaviour that might have been ignored or dismissed without comment in someone less richly endowed is observed and judged. Since his actions are interpreted by the onlookers as negative, unfriendly and snobby, they assume that he himself possesses those traits: 'His character was decided. He was the proudest, most disagreeable man in the world...' (p.10).

The citizens of Meryton have combined their observations of Darcy's behaviour with the deeply felt class consciousness of their society to reach this decision about his character. Their response partially reflects their own insecurities about both their physical appearance and their financial standing, as well as their awareness of their social status relative to his; they know that on all these grounds he has reason to feel superior and so assume that he does.

Close to two centuries after Austen described Darcy and the assumptions that others made about his character based on his behaviour, Tony Attwood noted that, 'The expressive body language of the person with Asperger's Syndrome can be misinterpreted... their manner be misperceived as aggressive, aloof or indifferent' (1998, p.63). Enlarging on this further in *The Profile of Friendship Skills in Asperger's Syndrome*, Attwood describes how 'they can also appear to be ill mannered or ungracious and somewhat autocratic' (2002, p.5).

Mr Bingley, who being 'lively and unreserved, danced every dance' (p.10), feels perturbed to see his usually competent friend 'standing about by [him]self in this stupid manner' (p.11). Obviously, in his experience, Darcy is usually more animated. Notice that Bingley does not express similar concern about his brother-in-law, Mr Hurst, whose dull-witted, alcoholic stupor is unchanging whatever the occasion! People on the spectrum 'can be relatively more relaxed and socially fluent with just one friend, but as with the saying "two's company and three is a crowd" they can become withdrawn and solitary when in a group' (Attwood 1998, p.48). Even more than for most of us, their social skills fluctuate depending on the company they keep.

In response to his friend's urging him to dance Mr Darcy replies, 'I certainly shall not. You know how I detest it, unless I am particularly well acquainted with my partner' (p.11). This is the first of several times when Darcy expresses a *strongly negative opinion about dancing*; an opinion that is highly unusual for his time and society, when dances and balls were generally regarded as fine entertainment. He has certainly been taught how to dance as , like riding, it would be considered a basic skill for someone of his social status. However, dancing, or moving rhythmically in time with others, does not seem to be pleasurable for him.

Nor is it for a number of those on the spectrum. Temple Grandin states that, 'I can keep rhythm moderately well by myself, but it is extremely difficult to synchronize my rhythmic motions with other people or with a musical accompaniment' (Grandin and Scariano 1986, p.26). She adds that she feels that many people on the spectrum have 'a right–left delay in body movements. Getting all the parts to work together is a monumental task' (1986, p.26). Similarly, Liane Holliday Willey, another author on the autistic spectrum, writes at length about her difficulties with ballet class as a six year old, when she reports that she 'could not for the life of me master the intricateness of it all; the coordination of bilateral movement it requires'

(1999, p.17); finally the director asked her mother to remove her 'in everyone's best interests' (p.18). The dance master hired to teach the little heir to
Pemberley would have had to persevere in the task in his own best interests!
Holliday Willey refers to practising for dance performances in high school
as 'bilateral torture', but describes how she persisted until:

> Eventually, after hours and hours of practice, I could make myself
> perform the dance steps with some degree of proficiency if there
> was someone in front of me to give me cues. Of course, this was not
> the only talent a dancer needed. Part one was memorizing the
> steps to the routine, part two was synchronizing them to music.
> Part one was a breeze compared to part two. I was always off beat.
> (1999, p.29)

Many of the adults with ASD whom I have met in my life either avoid dancing completely, stand stiffly if hauled onto the dance floor or else have
a rigid pattern of movements that they repeat without there being any
connection to the type of music being played.

Many readers at this point may be objecting, as images of the mesmeriz-
ing dance scenes in the 1995 BBC series fill their mind's eye. True, those
episodes are intricate and beautiful but they, and others like them, are in the
film versions. In the novel itself Austen says nothing specific about Darcy's
actual dancing skills the one and only time he does partner Lizzy. In addition, the systematic and orderly dances of the Georgian period do not
require either the smooth, fluid grace of the waltz or the strong rhythmic
sense needed to spontaneously create one's own movements as we do to
modern music. If we refer back to what Jane Austen actually wrote, Mr
Darcy does not dance off the page to meet us.

Besides strongly indicating that he does not enjoy dancing, the very
first time that he speaks in the novel, Mr Darcy also tells us how much he
prefers to be with people whom he already knows well. Therefore, he has
obviously not enjoyed the evening thus far as he has been surrounded by
strangers. When stressed and not comfortable it is a human tendency to
deride the situation responsible for those feelings. Many a student has
declared that a class is 'stupid' when, in actual fact, the content is above
them. Similarly, many a guest has been puzzled and bored by a sporting
event that is not in their tradition. (Offering in my defence that I am a prai-
rie-born Canadian raised on ice hockey and curling, I confess that I once fell
asleep during a cricket match at Lord's; behaviour close to sacrilege according to my Australian husband!) Seen from this perspective, Darcy's crisp

opinion that dancing at 'such an assembly as this...would be insupportable' (p.10) may reflect his insufficiencies more than those of the social event. Certainly class consciousness may account for a small part of his response, but probably not the bulk of it. Everyone tends to prefer situations where they feel skilled and in control.

Darcy ends this first conversation by saying to Bingley: 'Your sisters are engaged, and there is not another woman in the room, whom it would not be a punishment to me to stand up with' (p.11). Again, this edgy remark may not reflect so much on the women as on himself. Combining two things that do not come easily for him, dancing and exchanging social pleasantries with strangers, truly would be 'a punishment' and he is already feeling lacerated enough by having to remain in this complex, unfamiliar setting for so long.

Bingley, who has apparently seen Darcy primarily in situations where he is more at ease, doesn't understand how stressed his friend is and so interprets his answer as negative to the women. He, the younger and less dominant one in their friendship, is flourishing in this highly social situation so is unable to realize that it truly is challenging for the friend whom he so respects and admires. Therefore, he springs to the defence of the 'many pleasant girls' (p.11) who are present. Mr Darcy, who has probably kept his eyes on Bingley as one of the few familiar people in the confusing throng, has taken some notice of his twice-chosen partner and replies, '*You* are dancing with the only handsome girl in the room' (p.11).

Bingley immediately and enthusiastically offers to introduce his friend to a sister of this 'most beautiful creature' (p.11). At this point Darcy makes the comments that are pivotal to the entire novel as he damages Lizzy's pride and prejudices her against him:

> 'Which do you mean?' and turning round, he looked for a moment at Elizabeth, till catching her eye, he withdrew his own and coldly said, 'She is tolerable; but not handsome enough to tempt *me*; and I am in no humour at present to give consequence to young ladies who are slighted by other men. You had better return to your partner and enjoy her smiles, for you are wasting your time with me.' (p.12)

This is certainly not done with the graciousness and maturity of a Mr Knightley rescuing a Harriet Smith from a similar situation. We can almost hear that worthy gentleman saying, 'Badly done, Darcy. Badly done indeed.'

What could be behind such a rude and arrogant remark?

First of all, as Darcy himself states so accurately, he is in a sour, agitated state in 'no humour at present' (p.12) to be pleased by anything or anyone. He would not likely have taken note of the fact that there were more ladies than gentlemen present so hastily concludes that his attention is being directed towards someone not chosen by anyone as a desirable partner. He has latched onto that as a handy excuse to try and extricate himself from getting dragged into an even more uncomfortable situation. His response is uncivil but arises chiefly out of his own lack of ease with the entire assembly rather than being directed at Lizzy specifically. Attwood has noted four compensatory strategies that may develop in those with Asperger's syndrome to help them cope with their social difficulties.

> An alternative to internalizing negative thoughts and feelings is to externalize the cause and solution to feeling different. The [individual] can develop a form of over-compensation for feeling defective in social situations by denying that there is any problem, and by developing a sense of arrogance such that the 'fault' or problem is in other people. (2007, p.26)

Second, did Darcy truly *see* Elizabeth or merely *look* at her? This often compromised ability to see faces sounds unbelievable. However, in my experience, some on the autistic spectrum can literally walk past you with no indication that they recognize you from time spent together even earlier in the same day. When such children enter formal schooling at five years of age, it is often months, if ever, before they recognize and name everyone in their class.

Third, while agitated, he has made his remarks to his closest friend, who is urging him to do something he desperately wants to avoid. Rare is the person who has never murmured something to a confidante that they would not want the entire room to hear. 'Admirers of Darcy have long been at pains to account for his rudeness: supposing that he must be aware that she *can* overhear him, since she *does* overhear him, his barb seems to be deliberately launched' (Foster Stovel 2002, p.184). However, lack of awareness about what others know is a major deficit in autism. I do not believe that Darcy is aware that Elizabeth can hear him. Especially when agitated, many people on the spectrum have great difficulty with volume control. Lydia, Mrs Bennet, Mr Collins and Lady Catherine all repeatedly speak more loudly than is appropriate. In this one instance Darcy does as well. He is then too unaware of others to realize that he has been overheard. However, his reputation is now set. Lizzy spreads the story of his remark to her friends, while the entire community talks of his unusual, self-isolating behaviour.

Others beside Mrs Bennet, particularly if they also have daughters seeking a change in marital status, doubtless puzzle over and criticize him in their post-party discussions. Mrs Bennet declares 'with much bitterness of spirit and some exaggeration' (p.13) that he is:

> a most disagreeable man, not at all worth pleasing. So high and conceited that there was no enduring him! He walked here, and he walked there, fancying himself so very great! (p.13)

Again, telling of his constant walking is describing his behaviour, whereas saying that it is due to his inflated self-opinion is making an assumption. In part, Darcy's walking could be like that of a caged panther wanting to escape, but it may also indicate the basic difficulty he has joining already established groups. Again, professionally, I have observed similar walking by children with autism or Asperger's who did not have the social skills necessary to join in with others during unstructured playtime. The playground is for such children what a large dance in a strange town is for Mr Darcy: a noisy, constantly changing place with hundreds of fleeting social cues being sent by others. Frequently parents and teachers of children on the spectrum report that recess is the hardest subject in the curriculum for them. As adults, many with ASD simply avoid being in such group situations whenever possible or remain awkwardly on the fringes of them.

Once again, not letting her creations' behaviour form the sole basis for our gradually getting to know them, Jane Austen provides an authorial comment. In describing these two bachelors who have so aroused the marital hopes of Meryton and surroundings she tells us:

> Between [Bingley] and Darcy there was a very steady friendship, in spite of a great opposition of character – Bingley was endeared to Darcy by the easiness, openness, ductility of his temper, though no disposition could offer a greater contrast to his own, and though with his own he never appeared dissatisfied. On the strength of Darcy's regard Bingley had the firmest reliance, and of his judgement the highest opinion. In understanding Darcy was the superior. Bingley was by no means deficient, but Darcy was clever. He was at the same time haughty, reserved and fastidious, and his manners, though well bred, were not inviting. In that respect his friend had greatly the advantage. Bingley was sure of being liked wherever he appeared, Darcy was continually giving offence. (p.16)

Giving offence. Continually giving offence. This complaint about people with ASD persists through the centuries. English women attending Attwood's workshop for spouses in Coventry were quoted (2000, p.37) as saying:

> I had someone who said they would never invite my husband back because he was just so boorish and rude. He just wouldn't speak to other people, it was a very terse yes or no, he just sat there, he just put a blight on the whole party.

> My husband is two different people in that sense. Providing he's in his own home he can be the life and soul of the party. But take him out of the house to other situations; that he cannot cope with, head down etc.

> Mine is the same depending on whether he already knows the company, like his relatives.

Continually, but not intentionally, giving offence.

Following the dance, needless to say, Bingley and Darcy have very different recollections of the experience:

> Bingley had never met with pleasanter people or prettier girls in his life; every body had been most kind and attentive to him, there had been no formality, no stiffness, he had soon felt acquainted with all the room... Darcy, on the contrary, had seen a collection of people in whom there was little beauty and no fashion, for none of whom he had felt the smallest interest, and from none received either attention or pleasure. (p.16)

Notice that he saw 'a collection of people' and how none had stood out for him. He seems to have experienced the evening as a confusing blur of sensory experiences that he could not integrate.

Although he didn't feel interest in anybody, he certainly aroused interest. All are discussing this unusual man who did not talk. Mrs Bennet declares that:

> '...he is such a disagreeable man that it would be quite a misfortune to be liked by him. Mrs Long told me last night that he sat close to her for half an hour without once opening his lips.'
>
> 'Are you quite sure, Ma'am? – is not there a little mistake?' said Jane. – 'I certainly saw Mr Darcy speaking to her.'

> 'Aye – because she asked him at last how he liked Netherfield, and he could not help answering her; – but she said he seemed very angry at being spoke to.'
>
> 'Miss Bingley told me,' said Jane, 'that he never speaks much unless among his intimate acquaintance. With *them* he is remarkably agreeable.' (p.19)

From Miss Bingley's comment we once again learn that he acts very differently in small groups of familiar faces than he is able to in large crowds of strangers.

The accusation of pride is thrown at Darcy as a reason for his not speaking to Mrs Long. Mrs Bennet infers that the Longs' lack of a carriage doubtless made him feel her neighbour was beneath his attention. She herself does not have sufficient *theory of mind* to realize that, as a newcomer, he would be unlikely to know that. On the contrary, the chances of Darcy hearing of Mrs Long's mode of transportation are ludicrously small given that he is the least likely person to be engaged in trivial gossip of any sort. Like Mark Haddon's well-realized character, Christopher John Francis Boone, in *The Curious Incident of the Dog in the Night-time*, Darcy does not show competence at 'doing what is called chatting' (Haddon 2002, p.40), which is an essential skill in the initial stages of getting to know new people. Since he appears so capable in every other way, his lack in this area is attributed to pride:

> 'His pride,' said Miss Lucas, 'does not offend *me* so much as pride often does, because there is an excuse for it. One cannot wonder that so very fine a young man, with family, fortune, every thing in his favour, should think highly of himself. If I may so express it, he has a *right* to be proud.'
>
> 'That is very true,' replied Elizabeth, 'and I could easily forgive *his* pride, if he had not mortified *mine*.' (p.20)

Darcy has unwittingly injured her pride when she overheard him speaking to Bingley, so she retaliates by making his private comment very public indeed. This oft-told anecdote, coupled with his unexpectedly awkward social behaviour, produces a label for him. Labels should be used only if they help us understand someone; his label, unfortunately, leads to increased misunderstanding.

If we assume that the two sisters and the two friends attend all the same social events then, in the next fortnight, Darcy has five more opportunities to look at and begin to *see* Elizabeth. The five occasions are in much smaller groups as first the Bennet ladies pay a call to Netherfield and then they 'dined in company...four times' (p.22). Mr Darcy starts to be aware of 'the beautiful expression of her dark eyes' (p.23). When examining what attracts a man on the autistic spectrum to a woman:

> it appears to be a specific aspect of the partner's appearance that catches his interest. In my research, hair and eyes were highest on the preference list, Asperger syndrome produces a very narrow focus and rather than seeing the complete person, a specific part of her face or body may be the attraction. (Aston 2003, p17)

Similarly, Holliday Willey, when describing how she chose people to copy, wrote, 'I don't think I paid much attention to the overall appearance of the person. I remember being attracted to pieces of people's faces' (1999, p.23).

Gradually Darcy also becomes aware of Elizabeth's 'light and pleasing' figure and the 'easy playfulness' (p.23) of her manners. Therefore he:

> began to wish to know more of her, and as a step towards convers-ing with her himself, attended to her conversation with others. His doing so drew her notice. It was at Sir William Lucas's, where a large party were assembled.
>
> 'What does Mr Darcy mean,' said she to Charlotte, 'by listening to my conversation with Colonel Forster?' (p.24)

Darcy is betraying his difficulty with the subtle unwritten rules of non-verbal communication. If we wish to join a conversation we come close enough so that others are aware of our desire to join them. They then acknowledge us with their eyes as they alter their stance to include us in the group. Hovering nearby, close enough to listen but not close enough to sig-nal the desire to join, is generally regarded as eavesdropping. Again, his difficulty initiating conversation is apparent. In their book, *The Friendship Factor: Helping Our Children Navigate their Social World – and Why it Matters for their Success and Happiness*, Rubin and Thompson observe that, 'Breaking the ice can be a tough challenge for [people] of all ages. Some...push their way in, while others hover on the outskirts making no positive moves to establish contact' (2002, p.118).

Darcy follows up with another awkward half-measure as he approaches the pair of friends soon afterwards 'though without seeming to have any intention of speaking' (p.24). He exemplifies the recent insight from a man diagnosed as autistic in childhood that, '[S]triking up conversation with strangers is an autistic person's version of extreme sports' (Nazeer 2006, p.31). Darcy is a novice diver with his toes like talons gripping the end of the board as he hesitates above the social pool. The ladies have time to discuss his odd behaviour and their reaction before Lizzy turns to him, thus making the first move to converse. He manages to respond with one sentence and then the three-way conversation leads to Lizzy accompanying herself in song. When Mary succeeds her sister the younger Bennets and Lucases request that she play Scottish and Irish airs so that they and some officers may dance. Instead of joining the gaiety 'Mr Darcy stood near them in silent indignation at such a mode of passing the evening, to the exclusion of all conversation' (p.26).

Awkward as he finds the effort of initiating conversation, he prefers it to the even more torturous alternative of dancing. He:

> was too much engrossed by his own thoughts to perceive that Sir William Lucas was his neighbour, till Sir William thus began.
>
> 'What a charming amusement for young people this is, Mr Darcy! – There is nothing like dancing after all .– I consider it as one of the first refinements of polished societies.'
>
> 'Certainly, Sir; – and it has the advantage also of being in vogue amongst the less polished societies of the world. – Every savage can dance.' (p.26)

In this exchange Sir William shows more innate awareness of their society's beliefs than does the higher-ranking Mr Darcy. According to a historian of dance, 'in Regency as in former times, it was felt that the skill of a person's dancing expressed the quality of his or her soul or spirit' (Thompson 1999, p.3). Therefore, in the view of many, 'one measure of determining whether a man was truly a gentleman was by his ability to dance with confidence, to stand well, to move easily without calling attention to himself... Clumsiness, haughtiness and ostentatious display were to be avoided' (1999, p.3).

As a well-meaning host Sir William ignores the unwarranted savagery of his guest's abrupt reply:

> Sir William only smiled. 'Your friend performs delightfully;' he continued after a pause, on seeing Bingley join the group; – 'and I doubt not that you are an adept in the science yourself, Mr Darcy.'
>
> 'You saw me dance at Meryton, I believe, Sir.'
>
> 'Yes, indeed, and received no inconsiderable pleasure from the sight. Do you often dance at St James's?'
>
> 'Never.'

'Do you not think it would be a proper compliment to the place?'

'It is a compliment which I never pay to any place if I can avoid it.'

'You have a house in town, I conclude?'

Mr Darcy bowed.

'I had once some thoughts of fixing in town myself...but I did not feel quite certain that the air of London would agree with Lady Lucas.'

He paused in hopes of an answer; but his companion was not disposed to make any. (p.26)

In this brief and jerky conversation Darcy graphically shows the same difficulties with polite social interaction that were noted earlier in Mr Collins and Mr Bennet. Like Mr Collins, when he rejected the Bennet family's suggestion that he read a novel aloud, Mr Darcy is openly critical of the form of entertainment offered by his host. Most people quickly learn in early childhood that as a guest you do not say that the activities offered to you are 'boring', let alone imply that they would appeal to savages! Like Mr Bennet, Darcy also fails to take his conversational turn, leaving amiable Sir William waiting for a response. And yet again he speaks of his intense negative feelings about dancing.

Much as he dislikes it, however, he already likes Elizabeth more. Therefore, when Sir William chances on the gallant idea of offering him Lizzy as a partner in the next dance, 'though extremely surprised, [he] was not unwilling to receive [her]' (p.26). When Lizzy, much discomposed, starts to draw away, 'Mr Darcy with grave propriety requested to be allowed the honour of her hand' (p.26). The graveness and formality reminds us of Mr Collins; one has the sense that Darcy is relying on scripts taught by his dancing master. He would like to be with Elizabeth but has not yet been able to initiate an interaction smoothly.

He continues to focus on her even when another young lady is demanding his attention. Being long acquainted with Miss Bingley he is very verbal with her compared to the few stilted remarks he has managed to make to Elizabeth in the preceding two weeks. With the frankness for which people on the autistic spectrum are well known he tells her what he is thinking even though it is in complete disagreement with what she has just speculated. He states baldly, 'Your conjecture is totally wrong, I assure you' (p.27). His focus on one facial feature is revealed when he explains, 'I have been meditating on the very great pleasure which a pair of fine eyes in the face of a pretty woman can bestow' (p.27).

Since generally a man has learned not to sing the praises of the woman *he* is interested in to a woman whose interest is fixed on *him*, Miss Bingley assumes the best. Therefore she 'immediately fixed her eyes on his face, and desired he would tell her what lady had the credit of inspiring such reflections. Mr Darcy replied with great intrepidity, "Miss Elizabeth Bennet"' (p.27). Intrepidity? Or inability to tell one of those 'white lies' that remove some of the turbulence-causing rocks from the flow of social life?

Stunned and disappointed by this revelation, Miss Bingley immediately starts to tease him by making reference to the consequences of a serious attachment to the woman possessing those eyes. Darcy's response shows that he does have some ability to see the world from another's perspective (or at least from the perspective of this person, whom he knows well) as he responds, 'A lady's imagination is very rapid; it jumps from admiration to love, from love to matrimony in a moment. I knew you would be wishing me joy' (p.27).

Darcy's intense focus on Elizabeth continues when Jane's illness has brought her to stay at Netherfield:

> Elizabeth could not help observing…how frequently Mr Darcy's eyes were fixed on her. She hardly knew how to suppose that she could be an object of admiration to so great a man; and yet that he should look at her because he disliked her, was still more strange. (p.51)

Darcy does not seem to notice that his steady gaze is making another person uncomfortable. Similarly, Holliday Willey mentions that, when she was interested in people, 'I could stare at them all I liked, never thinking this might annoy them' (1999, p.23).

In this small house party, among some of his oldest friends, Mr Darcy is finally comfortable enough to initiate a conversation with Elizabeth. When Miss Bingley is playing a lively Scottish tune he draws near enough to Lizzy to ask her, 'Do not you feel a great inclination, Miss Bennet, to seize such an opportunity of dancing a reel?' (p.52). When she smiles but makes no verbal answer, he 'repeated the question, with some surprise at her silence'. Elizabeth responds with:

> a mixture of sweetness and archness in her manner which made it difficult for her to affront anybody; and Darcy had never been so

> bewitched by any woman as he was by her. He really believed, that were it not for the inferiority of her connections, he should be in some danger. (p.52)

He is powerfully attracted to her but, as an intelligent man of his period, is well aware that, in their society, their discrepancies of status and wealth would be viewed as incompatible. Marriage was more often a merger of property than of like minds and hearts.

Again, when among a small, familiar group of people, Darcy is able to demonstrate his awareness of social norms. Unlike others in the house party he is polite rather than deliberately rude. When he and Miss Bingley meet Elizabeth and Mrs Hurst out walking, the latter has no problem jettisoning her companion for a higher-status one:

> Then taking the disengaged arm of Mr Darcy, she left Elizabeth to walk by herself. The path just admitted three. Mr Darcy felt their rudeness and immediately said, – 'This path is not wide enough for our party. We had better go into the avenue.' (p.52)

That evening, in the calmness of the sitting room at Netherfield, Darcy again shows his ability to be perceptive when he correctly identifies the two motives Caroline Bingley could have for walking about the room with Elizabeth. Also, when Elizabeth strongly hints that she feels his weaknesses may be 'vanity and pride' (p.57), he counters by stating his own observations of his character. He reveals:

> 'I have faults enough, but they are not, I hope, of understanding. My temper I dare not vouch for. – It is I believe too little yielding – certainly too little for the convenience of the world. I cannot forget the follies and vices of others so soon as I ought, nor their offences against myself. My feelings are not puffed about with every attempt to move them. My temper would perhaps be called resentful. – My good opinion once lost is lost for ever. (p.58)

This tendency to be rigid, to lack flexibility or to be 'too little yielding', as Darcy describes it, is a common characteristic in many people on the autistic spectrum. Some have limited 'characterisation skills. They tend to be very black and white about who they like and who they don't like' (Attwood 2000, pp.2–3). In some cases this can mean that they make up their mind about a new acquaintance or idea quickly and permanently. The grandmother of a 13-year-old is quoted in the memoir, *Right Address... Wrong Planet*, as saying that his opinions 'can be firmly set in concrete in a nano second' (Barnhill 2002, p.186). Some with ASD hold a grudge for a much longer time than most people and do not modify their opinion to incorporate new experiences with whomever has offended them.

Darcy's attraction to Elizabeth is growing but, relying on reason rather than emotions, he views this as a negative. Therefore, he is relieved when he learns that she and her sister will be leaving.

> To Mr Darcy it was welcome intelligence – Elizabeth had been at Netherfield long enough. She attracted him more than he liked – and Miss Bingley was uncivil to *her* and more teazing than usual to himself. He wisely resolved to be particularly careful that no sign of admiration should *now* escape him, nothing that could elevate her with the hope of influencing his felicity; sensible that if such an idea had been suggested, his behaviour during the last day must have material weight in confirming or crushing it. Steady to his purpose, he scarcely spoke ten words to her through the whole of Saturday, and though they were at one time left by themselves for half an hour, he adhered most conscientiously to his book, and would not even look at her. (p.60)

Here we have an exquisite example of the complexity of the behaviour of those with mild autistic characteristics. As a desirable young bachelor Darcy is aware that marked attention from him may be interpreted by both the young woman and their society as possibly leading to something more permanent. His realization that even a 'sign of admiration' (p.10) may be misconstrued shows that he can appreciate the perspective of others cognitively when he is able to think it through at his leisure rather than in the flurry of real time. His intention is good and considerate; however his actions are not. Speaking barely ten words to a fellow house guest in the course of a day and then not even making eye contact when alone with the same guest is so extreme that it comes across as rude rather than considerate. He conveys his message awkwardly and blatantly rather than with smoothness or subtlety.

Before Elizabeth next meets this puzzling young man, another bachelor, who on the surface seems open and straightforward in contrast, provides her with additional information about him. George Wickham grew up with Darcy so his insights appear to have credibility as coming from one who has seen him both over time and in varying settings. In a confiding manner he shares his opinion that:

almost all [Darcy's] actions may be traced to pride; – and pride has often been his best friend. It has connected him nearer with virtue than any other feeling…

It [pride] has often led him to be liberal and generous, – to give his money freely, to display hospitality, to assist his tenants, and relieve the poor. Family pride, and *filial* pride, for he is very proud of what his father was, have done this. Not to appear to disgrace his family, to degenerate from the popular qualities, or lose the influence of the Pemberley House, is a powerful motive. He has also *brotherly* pride, which with *some* brotherly affection, makes him a very kind and careful guardian of his sister; and you will hear him generally cried up as the most attentive and best of brothers. (pp.81–2)

Although he skilfully defames Darcy's character, Wickham does give information that shows his childhood companion's positive traits as well. Accolades from someone who dislikes you can usually be taken as true! He describes Darcy as:

- liberal and generous
- display[ing] hospitality
- very proud of what his father was
- a very kind and careful guardian of his sister.

These descriptors indicate that his basic character is a positive and decent one. The main negative thing that Wickham has to say about Darcy is that 'almost all of his actions may be traced to pride'. The main proof he offers of this pride is 'his high and imposing manners' (p.78). Mr Wickham continues to give his opinions to Elizabeth:

but Mr Darcy can please where he chuses. He does not want abilities. He can be a conversible companion if he thinks it worth his while. Among those who are at all his equals in consequence, he is a very different man from what he is to the less prosperous. His pride never deserts him; but with the rich, he is liberal-minded, just, sincere, rational, honourable, and perhaps agreeable, – allowing something for fortune and figure. (p.82)

Again, ironically while criticizing the man, Wickham provides a list of many positive features. Truly, as Wickham says, Darcy 'does not want abilities'.

Unfortunately, his mild ASD characteristics mean that he is not always able to exhibit these abilities, especially when with large groups of people he does not know well. Often when this happens, as at the assembly ball, people observe his distinctive behaviour and attribute the cause to pride.

Elizabeth's next encounter with Darcy occurs at yet another ball. This time it is at the now familiar setting of Netherfield and he has met most of the people who are in attendance so he is better able to function socially. However, his interactions are still abrupt, and lacking in smoothness or grace.

> When those dances were over she [Lizzy] returned to Charlotte Lucas, and was in conversation with her, when she found herself suddenly addressed by Mr Darcy, who took her so much by surprise in his application for her hand, that, without knowing what she did, she accepted him. He walked away again immediately... (p.90)

In the heightened emotional state of approaching a young woman whom he finds attractive, Darcy neither greets her nor takes his leave verbally. Focused as he is on what he hopes to accomplish he also appears unaware that he has interrupted her ongoing conversation with someone else.

During Darcy's first dance with Elizabeth they have their longest private conversation thus far (obviously the music was at a lower volume than is common currently). Darcy's lack of proficiency with inconsequential social conversation is extremely noticeable:

> They stood for some time without speaking a word and she began to imagine that their silence was to last through the two dances, and at first was resolved not to break it; till suddenly fancying that it would be the greater punishment to her partner to oblige him to talk, she made some slight observation on the dance. He replied and was again silent. After a pause of some minutes she addressed him a second time with
>
> 'It is *your* turn to say something now, Mr Darcy – I talked about the dance, and you ought to make some kind of remark on the size of the room or the number of couples.'
>
> He smiled, and assured her that whatever she wished him to say should be said.
>
> 'Very well. – That reply will do for the present. – Perhaps by and bye I may observe that private balls are much pleasanter than public ones. – But *now* we may be silent.'
>
> 'Do you talk by rule then, while you are dancing?'

'Sometimes. One must speak a little, you know. It would look odd to be entirely silent for half an hour together, and yet for the advantage of *some*, conversation ought to be so arranged as that they may have the trouble of saying as little as possible.' (p.91)

Once again Darcy's difficulties with conversation are noted but erroneously attributed. His unexpected unfamiliarity with the broader expectations of a social dance is revealed when he asks if people usually talk while executing the figures. During these English country dances 'young people were expected to have on hand a repertoire of light conversation, with which to pass the time during the dance while they stood inactive' (Thompson 1999, p.6). To most this was 'a welcome opportunity to talk and flirt' (1999, p.2) despite the fact that, when being taught the dances, this was discouraged by 'many dancing masters, who preferred attentive silence' (1999, p.2). Darcy does not seem to have noticed that the stricture for silence he learned as a student is not followed by adults in a real-life setting. His comment may also indicate how he prefers to focus on his footwork. Especially when preparing for or performing a motor movement that requires concentration or is subtly challenging for them, many people on the spectrum prefer not to converse at the same time. I have heard of one young man with mild ASD who, while skating, abruptly told his date to stop talking to him so he could concentrate on his strides.

While the dance continues Elizabeth makes a rather extraordinary comment, stating 'archly' that she and Darcy are similar:

'...for I have always seen a great similarity in the turn of our minds.
– We are each of an unsocial, taciturn disposition, unwilling to speak, unless we expect to say something that will amaze the whole room, and be handed down to posterity with all the eclat of a proverb.'

'This is no very striking resemblance of your own character, I am sure,' said he. 'How near it may be to *mine*, I cannot pretend to say. – *You* think it a faithful portrait undoubtedly.'
'I must not decide on my own performance.'
He made no answer, and they were again silent... (p.91)

Lizzy's theory is that he will speak only if he can impress others with his intelligence. Perhaps Elizabeth is including herself in this hypothesis to make it less saucy. She is not unsocial but she is proud of her intelligence and wit so does like to say things that will 'amaze the whole room'. Darcy certainly interprets her statement literally and immediately recognizes that her character is far from taciturn. In a ballroom setting, unlike earlier in the Netherfield sitting room, he cannot maintain this type of semi-flirtatious and confusing play with words so falls into silence yet again.

When Elizabeth mentions that she has met Wickham, Darcy's expression changes as 'a deeper shade of hauteur overspread his features, but he said not a word' (p.92). When he eventually speaks his response indicates that he is aware that the other possesses a social ease that he himself does not: 'Mr Wickham is blessed with such happy manners as may ensure his making friends – whether he may be equally capable of *retaining* them, is less certain' (p.92). When Lizzy pointedly stresses that Wickham is suffering due to losing Darcy's friendship he 'made no answer' (p.92).

At this point they are spoken to by Sir William Lucas, who glances at Jane and Bingley as he alludes to 'a certain desirable event' (p.92). Mr Darcy's ability to follow Sir William's eye gaze and draw the correct inference is an indication that he is at the very mild end of the autistic spectrum. He does, however, take a few extra seconds to process the information so there is yet another noticeable pause before he recovers sufficiently to remember that he is conversing with his dance partner:

> 'Sir William's interruption has made me forget what we were talking of.'
>
> 'I do not think we were speaking at all. Sir William could not have interrupted any two people in the room who had less to say for themselves. – We have tried two or three subjects already without success, and what we are to talk of next I cannot imagine.'
>
> 'What think you of books?' said he, smiling.
>
> 'Books – Oh! no. – I am sure we never read the same, or not with the same feelings.'
>
> 'I am sorry you think so; but if that be the case, there can at least be no want of subject. We may compare our different opinions.'
>
> 'No – I cannot talk of books in a ball-room.' (p.93)

In an attempt to initiate conversation Darcy falls back on the old standard 'Have you read any good books lately?' without realizing that different topics are appropriate for different settings. Comparing opinions on literature or essays can be a rather serious and complex task, not to be undertaken in the midst of a cheerful and ever-changing dance. Although Mary would doubtless have been happy to converse with him on the subject, this Bennet sister is not!

Lizzy, however, lets Darcy know that she is wrestling with a different intellectual challenge as she tells him that she is trying to make out his character. She disclaims success, saying, 'I do not get on at all. I hear such different accounts of you as puzzle me exceedingly' (p.93). The fictional Lizzy joins thousands of people over the centuries who have puzzled over why a person of intelligence with so many abilities will also have unexpected areas of weakness involving seemingly 'simple' things. In this novel how can a man who is capable of managing a great estate be so awkward when approaching a woman at a dance? In our day-to-day world why would someone who has the verbal skills to teach calculus or expound at length on quantum physics have such difficulty having a chat while dining or while waiting in line at the supermarket? The juxtaposition of the image of a puzzle with autism is a widespread and recurring one. Many decades after Jane Austen penned these words for Elizabeth, puzzle pieces form the logos of autism societies adorn book covers and have even been made into attractive silver jewellery as a fundraiser.

As Lizzy continues to try to piece together the perplexing puzzle that is Mr Darcy, her sister, Jane, adds further snippets of information from Mr Bingley, whom she says 'will vouch for the good conduct, the probity and honour of his friend' (p.95). Such characteristics of uprightness and honesty are indeed among the valued traits associated with the high-functioning end of the autistic spectrum.

The rest of the ball brings Lizzy 'little amusement' as she is caught between two admirers at varying points along the spectrum. One approaches her too closely while the other hovers at a slight distance:

> She was teazed by Mr Collins, who continued most perseveringly
> by her side, and though he could not prevail with her to dance with
> him again, put it out of her power to dance with others... She was at
> least free from the offence of Mr Darcy's further notice; though
> often standing within a very short distance of her, quite disengaged,
> he never came near enough to speak. (p.102)

Neither young man is able to judge the socially appropriate proximity nor how to best win her interest and affection.

As the ball drags to an end with Mrs Bennet manoeuvring to be the last family to leave, neither Mr Darcy nor Mr Bennet is able to contribute anything to make the situation less awkward: 'Darcy said nothing at all. Mr Bennet, in equal silence, was enjoying the scene' (p.103).

Elizabeth and Darcy do not meet again for some months until their visits to Rosings accidentally coincide. Elizabeth is visiting her friend, Charlotte, now married to her paternal cousin, Mr Collins. Mr Darcy and one of his maternal cousins, Colonel Fitzwilliam, pay a courtesy call to the ladies at the parsonage in Hunsford:

> Mr Darcy looked just as he had been used to look in Hertfordshire, paid his compliments, with his usual reserve, to Mrs Collins; and whatever might be his feelings towards her friend, met her with every appearance of composure.
>
> Elizabeth merely curtseyed to him, without saying a word.
>
> Colonel Fitzwilliam entered into conversation directly with the readiness and ease of a well-bred man, and talked very pleasantly; but his cousin, after having addressed a slight observation on the house and garden to Mrs Collins, sat for some time without speaking to any body. At length, however, his civility was so far awakened as to enquire of Elizabeth after the health of her family. (p.171)

Darcy's social awkwardness is in sharp contrast with the 'readiness and ease' with which his cousin is able to chat with people he has never met before. Both Elizabeth Bennet and her creator, Jane Austen, attribute this to the Colonel's character and education, with no realization that he is fortunate enough to be 'neuro-typical', to use the expression created by those at the high-functioning end of the autistic spectrum to refer to the majority of us. The phrase 'with his usual reserve' indicates that Darcy's facial expression conveys limited, if any, emotion or pleasure at meeting Charlotte, Maria and Elizabeth again. Limited facial affect, as mentioned before, is a characteristic of some people on the spectrum.

The two households gather for an evening at Rosings. With four people on the spectrum present it is far from being a sparkling group so Colonel Fitzwilliam and Elizabeth are naturally drawn to each other in order to enjoy a stimulating, animated conversation. Lady Catherine 'did not scruple to call out' (p.173), rudely demanding to know what they were discussing. She also insensitively tells Lizzy she could practise on the pianoforte in the companion's room where she 'would be in nobody's way' (p.173). Mr Darcy 'looked a little ashamed of his aunt's ill breeding [but] made no answer' (p.173).

It is extremely positive to note that Mr Darcy is able to recognize such lapses in socially appropriate behaviour when they occur in another. Once again he does at least register the error but he does not know how to intervene quickly to improve the situation. In her chapter in the book *Stress and Coping in Autism*, Diane Twachtman-Cullen refers to the speed or 'multifaceted process of handling information in real time' (2006, p.309), and how it adds to the complexity of a conversation for those with ASD. She points out that the 'deceptive simplicity with which information processing takes place in neurotypical people belies its complex and multidimensional nature' (p.308).

As Darcy joins his cousin and Elizabeth around the piano she starts to tease him about the poor first impression he made when he was among strangers in Hertfordshire:

> 'Pray let me hear what you have to accuse him of,' cried Colonel Fitzwilliam. 'I should like to know how he behaves among strangers.'
>
> 'You shall hear then – but prepare yourself for something very dreadful. The first time of my ever seeing him in Hertfordshire, you must know, was at a ball – and at this ball, what do you think he did? He danced only four dances! I am sorry to pain you – but so it was. He danced only four dances, though gentlemen were scarce; and, to my certain knowledge, more than one young lady was sitting down in want of a partner. Mr Darcy, you cannot deny the fact.'
>
> 'I had not at that time the honour of knowing any lady in the assembly beyond my own party.'
>
> 'True; and nobody can ever be introduced in a ballroom. Well, Colonel Fitzwilliam, what do I play next? My fingers wait your orders.'
>
> 'Perhaps,' said Darcy, 'I should have judged better, had I sought an introduction, but I am ill qualified to recommend myself to strangers.'
>
> 'Shall we ask your cousin the reason of this?' said Elizabeth, still addressing Colonel Fitzwilliam. 'Shall we ask him why a man of sense and education, and who has lived in the world, is ill qualified to recommend himself to strangers?'
>
> 'I can answer your question,' said Fitzwilliam, 'without applying to him. It is because he will not give himself the trouble.' (p.175)

Darcy shows significant self-knowledge as he recognizes that he is 'ill qualified to recommend himself to strangers', and as he pinpoints his difficulty with conversation in particular. This awareness is superior to that of the other characters with ASD in the novel, and is a positive indicator that his skills will continue to develop and improve over time. However, he is blamed for his difficulties. People with obvious physical and mental disabilities are not held to be responsible for their shortcomings; however, the milder the difficulties the less visible their causes are to outsiders – hence they are seen as something occurring by choice or lack of effort. In their groundbreaking book *Shadow Syndromes: The Mild Forms of Major Mental Disorders that Sabotage Us*, John J. Ratey and Catherine Johnson write that:

> Until very recently parents, teachers, friends, neighbours, spouses, colleagues – all of us, in short – have viewed social awkwardness as entirely a matter of character. Bad character, we assume, or bad upbringing. We speak of social 'skills' as if social niceties were easily acquired and simple abilities, like riding a bike or driving a car: capabilities any reasonably well-put-together person can readily pick up. (1997, p.215)

Darcy is much more than 'reasonably well-put-together'! He was introduced to us as a 'fine, tall person' with 'handsome features' (p.10), seemingly blessed with everything that one could want in life. He has no apparent physical disabilities. He can talk, so why doesn't he? During this discussion Darcy himself shows significant insight into the subtle nature of his difficulties and tries to explain it to these two people whose good opinion he values:

> 'I certainly have not the talent which some people possess,' said Darcy, 'of conversing easily with those I have never seen before. I cannot catch their tone of conversation, or appear interested in their concerns, as I often see done.' (p.175)

Here he comes right to the heart of his difficulties but Elizabeth discounts his observations by attributing his lack of proficiency to the same cause as her standard of play on the pianoforte: 'I have always supposed it to be my own fault – because I would not take the trouble of practising' (p.175).

Sadly, even his congenial cousin does not recognize how truly challenging social interactions in large groups are for Darcy. Since the Colonel agrees with Lizzy that Darcy is a man of 'sense and education' (p.175), and since he has seen his cousin behave quite differently in small family groups, he also attributes this conversational deficiency to not bothering to take the trouble. This is akin to telling someone with a hearing loss to 'listen' or someone with limited vision to 'look'. That Darcy's puzzling and seemingly inconsistent behaviour has a possible neurological component will not be recognized until long in the future. In the meantime he and others like him will be blamed for their disability.

Ironically, Darcy continues to seek out Lizzy's company but then be unable to be companionable. There are more and more examples of how extremely challenging initiating conversation is for him. Numerous times he comes to call but then 'seem[s] in danger of sinking into total silence' (p.177). The exhausting role of lobbing conversational topics into the void falls totally on Elizabeth; sometimes Darcy returns them, but more often he does not. When joined by Charlotte and Maria he participates even less, 'sitting a few minutes longer without saying much to any body' (p.179):

> 'What can be the meaning of this!' said Charlotte, as soon as he was gone. 'My dear Eliza he must be in love with you, or he would never have called on us in this familiar way.'
>
> But when Elizabeth told of his silence, it did not seem very likely, even to Charlotte's wishes, to be the case... But why Mr Darcy came so often to the Parsonage, it was more difficult to understand. It could not be for society, as he frequently sat there ten minutes together without opening his lips; and when he did speak, it seemed the effect of necessity rather than of choice – a sacrifice to propriety, not a pleasure to himself. He seldom appeared really animated. Mrs Collins knew not what to make of him. Colonel Fitzwilliam's occasionally laughing at his stupidity, proved that he was generally different, which her own knowledge of him could not have told her; and as she would have liked to believe this change the effect of love, and the object of that love, her friend Eliza, she sat herself seriously to work to find it out... He certainly looked at her friend a great deal, but the expression of that look was disputable. It was an earnest, steadfast gaze, but she often doubted whether there were much admiration in it, and sometimes it seemed nothing but absence of mind. (pp.179–81)

Darcy's limited facial affect puzzles Mrs Collins, who is trying to work out his feelings. He 'seldom appeared really animated' (p.180) and, although he looked at Elizabeth often, 'the expression of that look was disputable' (p.181). Indeed his expression is so close to blank that it appears to be 'nothing but absence of mind' (p.181). Even his close friend and cousin, Colonel Fitzwilliam, laughs and comments about his behaviour, 'prov[ing] that he was generally different' (p.180). All the emotional wrestling with himself that Darcy is experiencing occurs inside himself, while he appears almost catatonic to outside observers.

Given that he shows so little enjoyment in her company Lizzy is startled when he appears to be seeking it outdoors as well as in.

> More than once did Elizabeth in her ramble within the Park, unex- pectedly meet Mr Darcy. – She felt all the perverseness: of the mischance that should bring him where no one else was brought; and to prevent it ever happening again, took care to inform him at first, that it was a favourite haunt of hers. – How it could occur a sec- ond time therefore was very odd! – Yet it did, and even a third. It seemed like wilful ill-nature, or a voluntary penance, for on these occasions it was not merely a few formal enquiries and an awkward pause and then away, but he actually thought it necessary to turn back and walk with her. He never said a great deal, nor did she give herself the trouble of talking or of listening much; but it struck her in the course of their third rencontre that he was asking some odd unconnected questions... (p.182)

Yet again, he 'never said a great deal' and what conversation he does initiate consists of 'odd unconnected questions'.

Elizabeth has a more appealing companion for a stroll when Colonel Fitzwilliam joins her. In a polite but indirect way he skilfully manages to inform her that, since 'younger sons cannot marry where they like' (p.183), he is not able to pursue her romantically. The feelings of both are thus pro- tected and they are able to joke in a lighthearted manner about 'the usual price of an Earl's younger son' (p.184). This is adroitly done in comparison with the silent treatment Darcy relied on at Netherfield when he also did not want to inadvertently raise the hopes of the same young woman. Both cousins recognized the message that needed to be conveyed but only one could do it smoothly and politely.

Since Colonel Fitzwilliam is talkative he unwittingly discloses informa- tion that adds to the puzzling collection of pieces Elizabeth is amassing about his cousin. He tells her that they have lingered longer at Rosings than originally planned when, in response to her query as to whether they are leaving Kent on Saturday, he answers, 'Yes – if Darcy does not put it off again. But I am at his disposal. He arranges the business just as he pleases' (p.183). The conversation then wanders to Darcy's desire to have his own way, and the type of care that he takes of his sister and his friends. The Colo- nel shares that Darcy 'congratulated himself on having lately saved a friend from the inconveniences of a most imprudent marriage' (p.185). Lizzy immediately infers that the story he relates refers to her beloved sister and Bingley.

> After watching her a little, Fitzwilliam asked her why she was so thoughtful.
>
> 'I am thinking of what you have been telling me,' said she. 'Your cousin's conduct does not suit my feelings. Why was he to be the judge?'
>
> 'You are rather disposed to call his interference officious?'
>
> 'I do not see what right Mr Darcy had to decide on the propriety of his friend's inclination, or why, upon his own judgment alone, he was to determine and direct in what manner that friend was to be happy.' (pp.185–6)

This tendency to come across as controlling, bossy or officious, and to think that you know what is best for another is common among people at the high-functioning end of the autistic spectrum. Attwood has observed that, in their friendships, there is a 'tendency to impose or dictate the activity... desire to have complete control' (1998, p.30). Many readers and commentators have speculated as to why such opposites as Darcy and Bingley have such a strong friendship. Attwood has noted that many children on the spectrum play with 'much younger kids who they can often boss' (2000, p.7), so one possibility is that, as a less self-confident, nouveau riche man with an amiable disposition, Bingley has not objected to being guided, indeed directed, by Darcy, who is six years his senior. Others closer to his age or rank may have resisted him more.

Elizabeth's new knowledge about how Darcy has prevented Jane's chance for marriage understandably does not augur well for him when he attempts to secure his own! But then he does not prepare the way well for himself either as he comes in the late evening in a hurried and agitated way. Not for him the careful selection of an idyllic setting and a romantic build-up to the actual proposal. The key problem, of course, is that he has not been thinking of her feelings but only of his own:

> to her utter amazement, she saw Mr Darcy walk into the room. In an hurried manner he immediately began an enquiry after her health, imputing his visit to a wish of hearing that she were better. She answered him with cold civility. He sat down for a few moments, and then getting up walked about the room. Elizabeth was sur-

prised, but said not a word. After a silence of several minutes he came towards her in an agitated manner, and thus began.

'In vain have I struggled. It will not do. My feelings will not be repressed. You must allow me to tell you how ardently I admire and love you.' (p.189)

Besides not in any way setting the stage for his proposal, Darcy is so focused on what he plans to do that he does not notice that he is greeted only with 'cold civility' and then silence. He is not able to read Elizabeth's expression or body language.

Elizabeth's astonishment was beyond expression. She stared, coloured, doubted, and was silent. This he considered sufficient encouragement, and the avowal of all that he felt and had long felt for her, immediately followed. He spoke well, but there were feelings besides those of the heart to be detailed, and he was not more eloquent on the subject of tenderness than of pride. His sense of her inferiority – of its being a degradation – of the family obstacles which judgement had always opposed to inclination, were dwelt on with a warmth which seemed due to the consequence he was wounding, but was very unlikely to recommend his suit...

...roused to resentment by his subsequent language, she lost all compassion in anger. She tried, however, to compose herself to answer him with patience, when he should have done. He concluded with representing to her the strength of that attachment which, in spite of all his endeavours, he had found impossible to conquer; and with expressing his hope that it would now be rewarded by her acceptance of his hand. As he said this, she could easily see that he had no doubt of a favourable answer. He *spoke* of apprehension and anxiety, but his countenance expressed real security. (p.189)

Seemingly too overwhelmed by his conflicting emotions to be aware of the distinction between talking to himself and talking to Elizabeth he says aloud all the arguments about her 'inferiority' due to 'family obstacles' that he has been using to try to convince himself against the very proposal he is in the midst of making. Essentially he has launched into a monologue that he has been repeating in his own head. The already quoted insight from Tony Attwood about the lack of an 'off' switch applies to both Collins and Darcy. Mr Darcy certainly shows no realization of how his concerns sound from Lizzy's perspective as he appears to have 'no doubt of a favourable answer' (p.189). 'Elizabeth has pride; she is a challenge, another strong personality, a mental equal. It does not occur to Darcy, however, that he must win her. He assumes, in his conceit, that she would be overjoyed by an offer from *him*' (Paris 1978, p.137).

In this lack of awareness of her perspective his proposal echoes the earlier one by Mr Collins. As Nora Foster Stovel writes in her essay in *The Talk in Jane Austen*, 'Even their proposals are parallel in some ways, as both detail their reasons for or against marrying' (2002, p.190). However, three major differences indicate that Darcy is in the much milder range of the autistic spectrum than is Mr Collins.

1. First of all, this time of heightened emotion is the only occasion when Darcy slips into a monologue, whereas most of Mr Collins's communication falls into this pattern.

2. Second, as Mann points out in her article on proposals, 'At least Mr Darcy began with his violent love, an improvement over Mr Collins, who only remembered his at the last moment' (2002, p.209).

3. Third, following Elizabeth's initial rejection, '[w]hile Collins changes the object of his attentions and proposals with alacrity...Darcy stands firm in both his affections and his intentions' (Foster Stovel 2002, p.190).

As he absorbs her unexpected refusal, Mr Darcy 'seemed to catch her words with no less resentment than surprise' (p.190). Once *he* had decided on marriage as a course of action it does not seem to have entered his head that *she* would not agree to it. If guided by reason and consideration of the financial and social benefits then her acceptance was the only possible, rational and sensible response. The fact that she might have any objections to him as a person was not conceivable. As Paris has noted:

> At the time of [this] first proposal, Darcy believes Elizabeth 'to be wishing, expecting [his] addresses' (III, xvi). Darcy's arrogance is partly responsible for this gross error, but he has also been misled by Elizabeth, who expresses her dislike under the guise of raillery. 'My manners,' says Elizabeth, 'must have been at fault, but not intentionally I assure you' ... In almost every exchange between them in the first half of the novel Darcy and Elizabeth misinterpret each other. He fails to understand her hostile and she his attentive behavior. (1978, p.108)

Therefore, both characters are in shock at this point: she by his proposal and he by her rejection of it.

Ironically, Darcy is the one to accuse Elizabeth of making 'little endeavour at civility' (p.190). He is stunned to be told in his turn that she has felt offended and insulted by his uncivil method of proposing. His response is to emphasize that 'disguise of every sort is my abhorrence' (p.192). Since honesty, to the point of being uncomfortable even with white or social lies, is a fundamental characteristic of those on the spectrum, Darcy does not realize that it would have been more diplomatic, while still honest, not to itemize every detail of his struggles and concerns about connecting himself with the Bennet family.

Elizabeth now uses an expression that astonishes Darcy into recognizing how he had phrased his proposal in an inept and insulting manner; she refers to his failure to behave in 'a more gentleman-like manner' (p.192). This pierces his self-image and propels him forward into the process of realizing that others view him differently than he does himself:

> She saw him start at this, but he said nothing…his astonishment was obvious; and he looked at her with an expression of mingled incredulity and mortification. She went on.
>
> 'From the very beginning, from the first moment I may almost say, of my acquaintance with you, your manners impressing me with the fullest belief of your arrogance, your conceit, and your selfish disdain of the feelings of others, were such as to form that groundwork of disapprobation, on which succeeding events have built so immoveable a dislike; and I had not known you a month before I felt that you were the last man in the world whom I could ever be prevailed on to marry.' (p.193)

Arrogance. Conceit. Selfish disdain of the feelings of others. These are strong words and stunning blows to a man who has felt that he behaves honourably, honestly and appropriately in all situations. He is unaware that his limited conversation, his discomfort meeting new people, as well as his forceful if well-meant guidance and advice, have led others to attribute such negative characteristics to him. Overwhelmed by this information and Lizzy's unexpected rejection of the proposal he has wrestled with for so long, he cannot fully and quickly process so many words and emotions in order to formulate a response in the heat of the moment. He essentially bolts from the room as he mouths a scripted phrase that could be used appropriately on many other occasions: 'Forgive me for having taken up so much of your time, and accept my best wishes for your health and happiness' (p.193).

Sarah Emsley writes regarding this closing statement, 'The apology may be narrow – he does not apologize for anything he has said or for injuring her feelings, but his wish for her welfare shows that he can pay attention to what is apart from himself' (2005, p.93). I interpret this differently as I don't think the 'forgive me' is an apology at all but rather part of an over-learned phrase he reproduces in full just as some ASD children can recite entire film scripts. At this point I do not feel that Darcy is able to acknowledge that he has done anything wrong. Similarly, I believe that the wish for 'health and happiness' is simply parroted as part of that oft-used formal sentence without any genuine interest in her welfare at the moment. Darcy is too swamped by unfamiliar and unexpected emotions to be aware of anyone besides himself.

However, when he has had *time alone* to think, Darcy chooses to continue the exchange with Elizabeth and does so by giving her a lengthy letter the next day. Turning to written rather than oral communication is often used by people at the mild end of the autistic spectrum. Based on his professional experience with over 2000 people on the spectrum, Attwood notes: 'Although there can be a problem with talking about one's feelings, there is often eloquence that is quite remarkable in written or typed form' (1998, p.63). Similarly, Uta Frith and Francesca Happe, in their work on theory of mind, have noted that people on the autistic spectrum 'appear to do better with written rather than spoken communication, where the fast to and fro of mental state appraisal is avoided' (1999, p.7).

In his long and articulate letter, written after he has had some time to absorb Elizabeth's accusations, Darcy is more aware that what he is saying may injure her feelings and writes, 'when the following account of my actions and their motives has been read… If, in the explanation of them which is due to myself, I am under the necessity of relating feelings which may be offensive to yours, I can only say that I am sorry' (p.197). This rings true as a genuine apology.

With regard to Elizabeth's belief that he has ruined her sister's chance for marital happiness, Darcy explains that he honestly did not think that Jane reciprocated his friend's regard:

> I had not been long in Hertfordshire, before I saw, in common with others, that Bingley preferred your eldest sister to any other young woman in the country… I had often seen him in love before… I

observed my friend's behaviour attentively; and I could then perceive that his partiality for Miss Bennet was beyond what I had ever
witnessed in him. Your sister I also watched – Her look and manners
were open, cheerful and engaging as ever, but without any symptom
of peculiar regard, and I remained convinced from the evening's
scrutiny, that though she received his attentions with pleasure, she
did not invite them by any participation of sentiment – If *you* have
not been mistaken here, *I* must have been in error. Your superior
knowledge of your sister must make the latter probable. (p.197)

Darcy, although watching for facial expressions and behaviours that would
indicate affection, may not have taken into account that a woman in their
society would be unlikely to show these too openly in such a public venue,
particularly when surrounded by people who had known her since babyhood.
When writing about the eighteenth century's conventions in connection with
the visible manifestations of emotion, Juliet McMaster noted that:

> Reading the signs of love is particularly important, but particularly
> difficult, since according to a *different* set of conventions a woman is
> meant to conceal hers. Darcy, in his attentive reading of Jane Bennet,
> fails to take account of this different convention. (2001, p.97)

As someone mildly on the autistic spectrum Darcy was not likely to have
been able to pick up any subtle, fleeting and concealed signs of a developing
love. Also he was not allowing for Jane's personality, which is not that of
someone likely to throw herself at an eligible young man. Indeed, Charlotte
Lucas had already commented that Jane's placidity and lack of variance of
facial expression might make it difficult for another to realize that she cared
about them. Finally, of course, we do tend to see what we are looking for,
and Darcy did not want to think that Jane's emotions were involved. The
fact that in hindsight Darcy is acknowledging that another person's perspective might be superior to his own in this instance is a positive indication
that, when calm, he is able to be flexible enough to appreciate another's
point of view.

In addition to thinking that Jane was indifferent to Bingley, Darcy also
wished to protect him from 'the evils' of loving a woman with such a complex and repugnant family:

> The situation of your mother's family, though objectionable, was
> nothing in comparison of that total want of propriety so frequently,
> so almost uniformly betrayed by herself, by your three younger sis-

ters, and occasionally even by your father. – Pardon me. – It pains
me to offend you. But amidst your concern for the defects of your
nearest relations, and your displeasure at this representation of
them, let it give you consolation to consider that, to have conducted
yourselves so as to avoid any share of the like censure, is praise no
less generally bestowed on you and your eldest sister... (p.198)

For these dual reasons of social class and familial impropriety, Darcy, plus
the united forces of the Bingley sisters, persuaded Charles Bingley not to
return to Hertfordshire as he had intended. Like most people on the spectrum Darcy relies on factual and rational reasons for exerting his influence.
As Barbara Laughlin Adler pointed out in her article on 'Gendered argument in Austen's novels', 'not once does he express his "feelings" or
"heartfelt instincts" as reason for encouraging Bingley to give up on Jane'
(2002, p.171).

At this point in his letter of defence Darcy does allude to an action of his
own with which he is not comfortable: 'There is but one part of my conduct
in the whole affair, on which I do not reflect with satisfaction; it is that I condescended to adopt the measures of art so far as to conceal from him your
sister's being in town' (p.199). No wonder he is not at ease with this behaviour, as he had earlier said of himself that 'disguise of every sort is my abhorrence' (p.192). Honesty and precise facts are extremely important to people
with ASD so it is an indication of how mildly he is on the autistic spectrum
that he was able to participate in concealing information. However, considering the characters and motives of those involved, very likely this deceit
was suggested by the Bingley sisters so Darcy's role was more a sin of omis-
sion rather than telling an outright, direct lie.

Darcy then explains the complex and lengthy history of Wickham's
involvement with and betrayal of his family. He draws his letter to an end by
writing, 'You may possibly wonder why all this was not told you last night.
But I was not then master enough of myself to know what could or ought to
be revealed' (p.202). Unlike his formal, stilted ending to the verbal interview, this time his simple closing rings true and indicates the depth of his
feeling for Elizabeth: 'I will only add, God bless you' (p.203).

Elizabeth wanders in the lane for two hours reading and re-reading the
letter, while recalling memories that support Darcy's statements – particularly about Wickham and about her family's conduct. As she begins to
incorporate this new information into the picture that she is trying to create
of Darcy's character she realizes that:

proud and repulsive as were his manners, she had never, in the whole course of their acquaintance, an acquaintance which had latterly brought them much together, and given her a sort of intimacy with his ways, seen any thing that betrayed him to be unprincipled or unjust – any thing that spoke him of irreligious or immoral habits. That among his own connections he was esteemed and valued – that even Wickham had allowed him merit as a brother, and that she had often heard him speak so affectionately of his sister as to prove him capable of *some* amiable feeling. That had his actions been what Wickham represented them, so gross a violation of every thing right could hardly have been concealed from the world; and that friend-ship between a person capable of it, and such an amiable man as Mr Bingley, was incomprehensible. (pp.207–8)

Gradually she realizes that his 'proud and repulsive' manners are the only negative thing she actually knows about him. When back at Longbourn, and confiding to Jane about the proposal and some of what he shared in his letter, she notes, 'There certainly was some great mismanagement in the education of those two young men. One has got all the goodness, and the other all the appearance of it' (p.225). Many many other people at the mild end of the autistic spectrum have also been erroneously labelled as proud or rude when they are truly finding it difficult to initiate conversation or to rec-ognize people they have met only once.

Almost four months later, when travelling in Derbyshire with her Uncle and Aunt Gardiner, Elizabeth has the unplanned opportunity to tour Darcy's home, Pemberley, while he is expected to be absent. They are taken about by the housekeeper, Mrs Reynolds, who is 'a respectable-looking, elderly woman, much less fine, and more civil, than she had any notion of finding her' (p.246). As they progress through the rooms and admire the views, 'Mrs Reynolds, either from pride or attachments, had evidently great pleasure in talking of her master and his sister' (p.248). Her remarks are all positive and dwell on Darcy's many merits:

- 'I do not know who is good enough for him [to marry]' (p.248).

- 'I have never had a cross word from him in my life, and I have known him ever since he was four years old' (p.248).

- 'If I was to go through the world I could not meet with a better [master]. But I have always observed, that they who are good-natured when children, are good-natured when they grow up; and he was always the sweetest-tempered, most generous-hearted, boy in the world' (p.249).

- 'his son will be just like him [the senior Mr Darcy] – just as affable to the poor' (p.249).

- 'He is the best landlord, and the best master,' said she, 'that ever lived. Not like the wild young men now-a-days, who think of nothing but themselves. There is not one of his tenants or servants but what will give him a good name. Some people call him proud; but I am sure I never saw any thing of it. To my fancy, it is only because he does not rattle away like other young men' (p.249).

- 'Whatever can give his sister any pleasure, is sure to be done in a moment. There is nothing he would not do for her' (p.250).

Can these accolades co-exist with a diagnosis of mild autism? Certainly.

When Mrs Reynolds met little Master Fitzwilliam Darcy as a four-year-old child, their relationship would have been be quite formalized or scripted as she was no doubt a maid or in another less responsible position than she now holds. She would mainly have seen him with adults, whom most children on the spectrum find easier to relate to than their less predictable age peers. In his early years he was an only child. Unlike a modern, urban child who has to adjust to one group of children at school, another dozen or so in his neighbourhood, as well as still others in day care, on the sports field or in religious classes, the young Fitzwilliam Darcy usually had only one other child, George Wickham, as his main companion, supplemented by occasional visits from his handful of cousins. In the enclosed community at Pemberley he would not have been interacting with new people hourly as those of us who live and work in modern cities are expected to do. His days would have had a strong and predictable routine, which reduces stress for children on the spectrum. In his chapter in the book *Stress and Coping in Autism*, Tony Attwood notes that:

> Children with Asperger's syndrome may see the world as consisting of unconnected fragments (due to weak central coherence) and are often desperate to create and maintain order to avoid what appears to be chaos. Changes in routine can result in conspicuous confusion and distress. The children may try to avoid situations that are unfa-

miliar, that lack clear structure, or that are new because they have no anticipated script of events. (p.353)

I suggest that it is possible to eliminate all the diagnostic signs of Asperger's Syndrome in a particular child. When children are alone... they have no need of social or communication skills and can do what they want to do in their own way. The classic diagnostic signs of Asperger's syndrome have disappeared. (p.358)

Life as the heir to Pemberley 200 years ago would have been almost ideal to reduce the symptoms of a child with mild autism!

Mrs Reynolds is aware that some call her master proud but has never seen that herself. Since he has known her for over 20 years Darcy is doubt-less completely relaxed and comfortable in her presence, so she would not see the social awkwardness others have labelled as 'pride', but that may in large part arise from his mild autism. She then compares Darcy to other young men in their mid-twenties. Like many elderly women, whatever the century, she views that age group as often 'wild', and comments on how they 'rattle away' no doubt talking of their own interests and/or using the current slang in a way that makes them almost unintelligible. She has noticed Darcy's slight differences from them but, from her perspective, these are to be encouraged!

As Elizabeth gazes at a portrait of Darcy looking relaxed and smiling, these glowing comments from Mrs Reynolds coupled with the good taste of his home tip her feelings for him from negative to positive. Within minutes her more favourable disposition towards him is reinforced by his unex-pected appearance at his home a day earlier than expected. Initially each of them is startled and intensely embarrassed. Both are so overpowered by a mix of emotions that neither is capable of speaking coherently:

Their eyes instantly met, and the cheeks of each were overspread with the deepest blush. He absolutely started, and for a moment seemed immoveable from surprise; but shortly recovering himself, advanced towards the party, and spoke to Elizabeth, if not in terms of perfect composure, at least of perfect civility.

She had instinctively turned away; but, stopping on his approach, received his compliments with an embarrassment impossible to be overcome...and knew not what answer she returned to his civil enquiries after her family. Amazed at the alteration in his manner since they last parted, every sentence that he uttered was increasing her embarrassment; and every idea of the impropriety of her being found there, recurring to her mind, the few minutes in which they continued together, were some of the most uncomfortable of her life. Nor did he seem much more at ease; when he spoke, his accent had none of its usual sedateness; and he repeated his enquiries as to the time of her having left Longbourn, and of her stay in Derbyshire, so often, and in so hurried a way, as plainly spoke the distraction of his thoughts.

At length, every idea seemed to fail him; and, after standing a few moments without saying a word, he suddenly recollected himself, and took leave. (pp.251–2)

Elizabeth is once again totally puzzled by Darcy's behaviour; this time because it differs from what she has seen in Hertfordshire and Kent. 'Never in her life had she seen his manners so little dignified, never had he spoken with such gentleness... She knew not what to think, nor how to account for it' (p.252). In a few moments she experiences even more markedly different behaviour from him. As she wanders along the walk and through the woods with the Gardiners they spot Mr Darcy deliberately heading towards them:

With a glance she saw, that he had lost none of his recent civility; and, to imitate his politeness, she began, as they met, to admire the beauty of the place... Mrs Gardiner was standing a little behind; and on her pausing, he asked her, if she would do him the honour of introducing him to her friends. This was a stroke of civility for which she was quite unprepared; and she could hardly suppress a smile, at his being now seeking the acquaintance of some of those very people, against whom his pride had revolted, in his offer to herself... Elizabeth could not but be pleased, could not but triumph. It was consoling, that he should know she had some relations for whom there was no need to blush. She listened most attentively to all that passed between them, and gloried in every expression, every sentence of her uncle, which marked his intelligence, his taste, or his good manners...continually was she repeating, 'Why is he so altered? From what can it proceed? It cannot be for *me*, it cannot be for *my* sake that his manners are thus softened. My reproofs at Hunsford could not work such a change as this.' (pp.256–7)

In my opinion, Elizabeth is right. Her 'reproofs' alone, contrary to what many commentators have speculated, could not alone have caused such a dramatic change in Darcy's behaviour. Lizzy couldn't, but location could.

At Pemberley, Darcy is on familiar ground. He literally has the home field advantage. Not only does he know the place and the people who work there, but he knows who he is and how he is to behave in relation to each of them. However, even though Darcy is calm and composed overall on his own property, he still finds it difficult to initiate conversation with Elizabeth as she triggers such varied emotions: 'Mr Darcy took her [Mrs Gardiner's] place by her niece, and they walked on together. After a short silence, the lady first spoke' (p.256). Lizzy clarifies that 'she had been assured of his absence before she came' (p.256), to which he responds that he has ridden a day ahead of his guests. After telling her that the Bingleys are expected shortly he pauses, then tells her that his sister would like to meet her.

> They now walked on in silence; each of them deep in thought. Elizabeth was not comfortable; that was impossible; but she was flattered and pleased. His wish of introducing his sister to her, was a compliment of the highest kind... At such a time, much might have been said, and silence was very awkward. She wanted to talk, but there seemed an embargo on every subject. At last she recollected that she had been travelling, and they talked of Matlock and Dove Dale with great perseverance. (pp.256–7)

Naturally, after being greeted so hospitably by the owner of the property they are visiting, the Gardiners are at a loss to reconcile their experience of him with the criticisms they have heard earlier from their niece.

> The observations of her uncle and aunt now began: and each of them pronounced him to be infinitely superior to any thing they had expected. 'He is perfectly well behaved, polite, and unassuming,' said her uncle.
>
> 'There *is* something a little stately in him to be sure,' replied her aunt, 'but it is confined to his air, and is not unbecoming. I can now say with the housekeeper, that though some people may call him proud, I have seen nothing of it.' (p.257)

Aunt Gardiner, a very perceptive and socially astute woman, has noted the very slight formality with which Darcy converses and carries himself; the 'something a little stately...confined to his air'. Although Mr Collins and Mary are more obviously pedantic, Darcy may have a slight trace in his intonation pattern or choice of words. Or perhaps Mrs Gardiner is picking up on something slightly stiff or wooden in how he moves, the angle at which he carries his head or his range of facial expressions. Overall, however, such things are very subtle and seemingly unimportant, as both she and her husband feel welcomed and respected by him.

> 'I was never more surprised than by his behaviour to us. It was more than civil; it was really attentive; and there was no necessity for such attention. His acquaintance with Elizabeth was very trifling.'
>
> 'To be sure, Lizzy,' said her aunt, 'he is not so handsome as Wickham; or rather he has not Wickham's countenance, for his features are perfectly good. But how came you to tell us that he was so disagreeable?'
>
> Elizabeth excused herself as well as she could; said that she had liked him better when they met in Kent than before, and that she had never seen him so pleasant as this morning. (pp.257–8)

Poor Lizzy! More pieces to the puzzle. Ones that do not seem to fit with those she has already collected. She may feel as if she is actually working on two puzzles at once without realizing it.

The very next morning Darcy brings both Georgiana and Bingley to visit, which naturally amazes Elizabeth's aunt and uncle, who quickly draw the correct inference that Darcy must have 'a partiality for their niece' (p.260). Darcy in his own neighbourhood is comparatively relaxed. Now his features are composed like those Lizzy warmed to in his portrait rather than the 'frozen' expression interpreted as haughty, which he usually bore when he was out in company. He is able to be animated, showing much more affect than has been witnessed before:

> [Elizabeth] saw an expression of general complaisance, and in all that he said, she heard an accent so far removed from hauteur or disdain of his companions, as convinced her that the improvement of manners which she had yesterday witnessed, however temporary its existence might prove, had at least outlived one day... Never, even in the company of his dear friends at Netherfield, or his dignified relations at Rosings, had she seen him so desirous to please, so free from self-consequence, or unbending reserve as now... (p.263)

If the change in Darcy's demeanour was totally due to him taking to heart Lizzy's accusation of ungentlemanly behaviour then we would expect the change to be a permanent one around her whatever the setting. However, later on in the novel, when he is back among less compatible company at Longbourn, he will once again become awkward and quiet.

The good Gardiners naturally observe all they can, and canvass their friends in Lambton to learn more about this possible admirer of their beloved niece. Their confidants have 'nothing to accuse him of but pride', but 'acknowledged, however, that he was a liberal man, and did much good among the poor' (p.265). Yet again it is his facial expression, or lack thereof, rather than his actions, that has shaped people's opinion of him.

Just as the couple are getting a fresh start to correct the initial poor first impressions they each made on the other, Elizabeth receives the horrific news that Lydia has run off with Wickham. As she absorbs the full implications of her teenaged sister's disastrous action:

> Mr Darcy appeared. Her pale face and impetuous manner made him start, and before he could recover himself enough to speak, she, in whose mind every idea was superseded by Lydia's situation, hastily exclaimed, 'I beg your pardon, but I must leave you... I have not an instant to lose.'
>
> 'Good God! what is the matter?' cried he, with more feeling than politeness... (p.276)

How wonderful! He speaks 'with more feeling than politeness'! At long last Darcy is responding from an *emotional* rather than a *rational* point of view. He instantly recognizes that the non-verbal message conveyed by her 'pale face and impetuous manner' indicates that something is amiss. Having been oblivious to her facial expressions when he proposed, he is now beginning to tune in to them.

Once a servant is sent to fetch the Gardiners, Lizzy is 'unable to support herself' and looks 'so miserably ill' that Darcy continues to express great concern for her in 'a tone of gentleness and commiseration' (p.276). He wants to do something practical so offers to fetch her maid or a glass of wine. As she bursts into tears he stays with her 'in compassionate silence' (p.277). In all this he is showing awareness of her feelings and an appropriate level of empathy. At last Elizabeth is able to share the dreadful tidings that her youngest sister has gone off with the man he so despises. 'Darcy [is] fixed in astonishment' (p.277) when he hears that the fate from which he saved his sister has now befallen another. Lizzy adds in agitation:

> 'Had his character been known, this could not have happened. But it is all, all too late now.'
>
> 'I am grieved, indeed,' cried Darcy; 'grieved – shocked. But is it certain, absolutely certain?' (p.277)

As Elizabeth confirms the facts, she confides that she has 'not the smallest hope. It is in every way horrible!' (p.277), and reiterates that she should have made sure that the true facts about Wickham's past history were known to others. 'But I knew not – I was afraid of doing too much. Wretched wretched mistake!' (p.278).

These words penetrate deeply into Darcy's mind as he recognizes his own role in these disastrous events. He starts to move into a practical, problem-solving mode as he thinks of how to bring some degree of hope, or at least improvement, to the situation. As he will tell Lizzy weeks later, 'his resolution of following her from Derbyshire in quest of her sister, had been formed before he quitted the inn' (p.370). Unfortunately, however, as his focus shifts to a solution, he stops responding emotionally to Elizabeth and does not realize how she will interpret his apparent withdrawal:

> Darcy made no answer. He seemed scarcely to hear her, and was walking up and down the room in earnest meditation his brow contracted, his air gloomy. Elizabeth soon observed, and instantly understood it...and never had she so honestly felt that she could have loved him, as now, when all love must be vain...covering her face with her handkerchief, Elizabeth was soon lost to every thing else; and, after a pause of several minutes, was only recalled to a sense of her situation by the voice of her companion, who, in a manner, which though it spoke of compassion, spoke likewise restraint, said, 'I am afraid you have been long desiring my absence, nor have I any thing to plead in excuse of my stay, but real, though unavailing, concern. Would to heaven that any thing could be either said or done on my part, that might offer consolation to such distress...
> (p.278)

It does not occur to Darcy that his 'gloomy' air and the 'restraint' in his voice will lead Lizzy to the conclusion that any hope of a relationship between them has ended. On her side, despite blatant proof to the contrary, Lizzy has once again fallen into the error of believing that she can read character accurately, as she assumes that she has 'instantly understood' what Darcy must be thinking and feeling.

The true feelings with which Darcy was grappling are brought out almost a month later when Aunt Gardiner writes to Elizabeth to explain how he came to play such a pivotal role in the nuptials of Lydia and Wickham:

his conviction of its being owing to himself that Wickham's worth-lessness had not been so well known, as to make it impossible for any young woman of character, to love or confide in him. He generously imputed the whole to his mistaken pride and confessed that he had before thought it beneath him, to lay his private actions open to the world. His character was to speak for itself. He called it, therefore, his duty to step forward... Nothing was to be done that he did not do himself... It was owing to him, to his reserve, and want of proper consideration, that Wickham's character had been so misunderstood... (pp.321-2)

Like many on the spectrum Darcy has a strong sense of justice. By 'want of proper consideration' he is recognizing that he did not consider other people and the possibility that Wickham would again try to seduce an underage girl. He was thinking only of his own sister and not able to imagine others in a similar situation. Since Darcy sees the error as his, he feels that it must be rectified by him. He disregards the fact that others are implicated to some degree, including Elizabeth, who also did not warn other young women, Mr Bennet, who did nothing to protect his daughters from such predators, and of course the two principal players themselves, who must hold some responsibility for their actions.

After relaying the facts Mrs Gardiner shares some of her observations about Darcy, describing him as 'very obstinate' and adding, 'I fancy, Lizzy, that obstinacy is the real defect of his character after all. He has been accused of many faults at different times; but *this* is the real defect of his character after all' (p.325). Since Darcy is so determined to bear the cost and trouble of establishing the future Mr and Mrs Wickham, he is not able to appreciate that this solution is humiliating for some at least of the bride's relatives. Although Lydia's father will ultimately express relief that he needs to assume no financial responsibility for his daughter, her socially astute and benevolent uncle 'would most readily have settled the whole' (p.325). If sensitive to the pride and honour of such an admirable man as Mr Gardiner, Darcy could have agreed on a compromise that allowed each to bear some of the costs. However, he 'battled' until at last the good uncle 'was forced to yield, and instead of being allowed to be of use to his niece, was forced to put up with only having the probable credit of it, which went sorely against the grain' (p.325). Although he himself abhors deceit, Darcy has not noticed that he has put Mr Gardiner into the acutely uncomfortable position of having 'borrowed feathers' and receiving gratitude he does not feel he has earned. In this instance Darcy lacks the *theory of mind* to understand the issue of honour from another's perspective.

Despite this fault she terms obstinacy, Mrs Gardiner's overall opinion is very positive as she tells Lizzy how much she likes Darcy. She elaborates that, 'his behaviour to us has, in every respect, been as pleasing as when we were in Derbyshire. His understanding and opinions all please me; he wants nothing but a little more liveliness...' (p.325).

Darcy certainly doesn't exhibit any liveliness when he unexpectedly comes with Bingley to visit the Bennet sisters at Longbourn several weeks later. When Elizabeth ventures a glance at him she observes that, '[h]e looked serious as usual; and she thought, more as he had been used to look in Hertfordshire, than as she had seen him at Pemberley' (p.335). Now that he is away from the familiar safe setting of his own home, Darcy is again tending to be wooden and awkward. The 'serious' look again indicates the problem the rest of us have with interpreting limited facial affect. People with mobile faces that exhibit a range of emotions can remain quiet during a conversation and yet still participate in it in a positive way as their expressions show agreement, empathy, amusement or other feelings to reflect what the speakers are saying. Those on the spectrum are more likely to have an immobile face, which can be quite disconcerting to the speakers, who gradually start to feel that it indicates boredom or contempt.

> Darcy, after enquiring of her how Mr and Mrs Gardiner did, a question which [Elizabeth] could not answer without confusion, said scarcely anything. He was not seated by her; perhaps that was the reason of his silence; but it had not been so in Derbyshire. There he had talked to her friends, when he could not to herself. But now several minutes elapsed without bringing the sound of his voice; and when occasionally, unable to resist the impulse of curiosity, she raised her eyes to his face, she as often found him looking at Jane, as at herself, and frequently on no object but the ground. More thoughtfulness, and less anxiety to please than when they last met, were plainly expressed. (p.336)

Yet again Austen tells us that Darcy 'said scarcely anything'. Once out of his comfort zone he is still unable to initiate or respond to conversation in a smooth, natural manner. Admittedly conversing in a group dominated by Mrs Bennet with her triumph of having Lydia 'well married' (p.336), her barbs levelled against him for not befriending Wickham adequately, and her unnecessary and excessive invitations to shoot the Longbourn birds, would reduce many a young man to semi-speechlessness but Bingley at least manages to make the appropriate murmurs. His 'common politeness' (p.339) carries him through both the surface turbulence and complex undercurrents of this apparently set-piece social call.

> As soon as they were gone, Elizabeth walked out to recover her spirits; or in other words, to dwell without interruption on those subjects that must deaden them more. Mr Darcy's behaviour astonished and vexed her.
>
> 'Why, if he came only to be silent, grave, and indifferent,' said she, 'did he come at all?'
>
> She could settle it in no way that gave her pleasure.
>
> 'He could be still amiable, still pleasing, to my uncle and aunt, when he was in town; and why not to me? If he fears me, why come hither? If he no longer cares for me, why silent? Teazing, teazing, man! I will think no more about him.' (p.339)

Contrary to Lizzy's resolution to 'think no more about him' she will do precisely that for the rest of her life, while we readers continue to do so centuries afterwards!

On the following Tuesday, when the Bennets host a 'large party' (p.340) at their home, Elizabeth again witnesses Darcy unable to contribute to the flow of conversation. At the dining table:

> He was on one side of her mother. She knew how little such a situation would give pleasure to either, or make either appear to advantage. She was not near enough to hear any of their discourse, but she could see how seldom they spoke to each other, and how formal and cold was their manner, whenever they did. (p.340)

In this setting Darcy is beside a hostess who deliberately and rudely makes no effort to include him. While, in this instance, her lack of conversation seems to be by choice, his, like his female cousin's earlier in the novel, is more likely due to the difficulties many of those on the autistic spectrum have initiating and maintaining a conversation.

Elizabeth's hope to have a chance to converse with him is finally granted after the meal when he brings his coffee cup back to the table where she is seated, pouring for the guests. She seizes the opportunity to ask him about his sister. He replies to her two direct questions with equally direct answers, but neither is able to sustain the conversation beyond that: 'He stood by her, however, for some minutes, in silence; and at last...he walked away' (p.342).

While this potential couple manage to exchange only a few stilted sentences during the entire evening, the other young couple make eye contact, exchange welcoming smiles, sit together and spend the greater part of the evening enjoying each other's conversation. But then Jane, who stresses that she does not wish to be suspected of being in love with him, describes Bingley as being 'blessed with greater sweetness of address, and a stronger desire of generally pleasing than any other man' (p.343). Yet in Derbyshire, only six weeks earlier, Darcy had also behaved in such a way as to be described by Lizzy in similar phrases. Then she had noted his 'expression of general complaisance' and had seen him be 'so desirous to please' (p.263). If, as many critics and readers believe, Elizabeth's rebuke was the sole reason for his change then, why is the lesson learned from that rebuke influencing him less now? Or does this confirm, as noted in the Pemberley scenes, that not just Lizzy's analysis of his character but also the location influences Darcy's behaviour? Just as when he first came to the assembly ball the previous autumn, he is once again less able to demonstrate the conversational skills we consider as basic when he is away from home in a fluid social setting with a swirl of emotional undercurrents.

On this occasion Mr Darcy was able to approach Elizabeth over coffee but not initiate conversation. This does not bode well for anything more intimate and yet, approximately ten days later, after a brief visit to London, Darcy once again accompanies Bingley to visit the ladies of Longbourn. In the intervening time, however, his authoritarian and autistic aunt has descended on Elizabeth and been 'most seriously displeased' (p.358) by that young lady's refusal to promise she would not marry Darcy. She relates this unsatisfactory interview to her nephew, not realizing how differently he will interpret it. As he later tells Lizzy, her responses gave him hope as 'I knew enough of your disposition to be certain, that, had you been absolutely, irrevocably decided against me, you would have acknowledged it to Lady Catherine, frankly and openly' (p.367).

This hope is still not enough to help him over the hurdle of taking the major emotional risk of proposing again. Bingley, having successfully secured his own lady love, assists his friend when he 'proposed their all walking out' (p.365) and then manages to lag behind with his Jane. Kitty, too, leaves so that Elizabeth and Darcy are alone. Up until this point, 'Very little was said by either; Kitty was too much afraid of him to talk; Elizabeth was secretly forming a desperate resolution; and perhaps he might be doing the same' (p.365).

Given Darcy's difficulties with initiation, one wonders how many miles they might have paced if it had been left up to him to take advantage of this opportunity for private conversation. However, Elizabeth, 'while her courage was high' (p.365), takes the first step to move them from a polite to a personal level by thanking him for rescuing her youngest sister. Once the initial hurdle of beginning to communicate has been cleared, Darcy responds to the warm and unthreatening mood of the interaction and is able in a simple, direct and moving way to let Lizzy know that his 'affections and wishes are unchanged' (p.366) from the preceding April.

Once started and with the paralysing tension removed, Darcy converses like the intelligent, articulate man that he is when not stressed. Naturally this conversation and subsequent ones over the next few days centre around their history together...or not together as was more often the case. Both their attractions and their altercations are examined.

Darcy shows that he has experienced growth in his self-awareness as they discuss the manner of his initial proposal:

> The recollection of what I then said, of my conduct, my manners, my expressions during the whole of it, is now, and has been many months, inexpressibly painful to me. Your reproof, so well applied, I shall never forget: 'had you behaved in a more gentleman-like manner.' Those were your words. You know not, you can scarcely conceive, how they have tortured me; – though it was some time, I confess, before I was reasonable enough to allow their justice. (pp.367–8)

The mention of 'some time' is crucial as it points out the need for extra processing time that some individuals on the autistic spectrum require, particularly around social issues. Darcy's first proposal was in early April while this second and successful one occurs in early October, a gap of half a year. This passage also shows his difficulty with self-knowledge or being able to look at himself from someone else's viewpoint. Darcy had to be told very bluntly that his behaviour was inappropriate, and he had to face the severe consequence that he might lose the first woman whom he had ever considered making his wife before he could recognize his error. Initially overcome by 'bitterness of spirit' (p.368) and a desire to defend himself, he now appreciates receiving such clear feedback about his behaviour:

> dearest, loveliest Elizabeth! What do I not owe you! You taught me a
> lesson, hard indeed at first, but most advantageous. By you, I was
> properly humbled. I came to you without a doubt of my reception.
> You shewed me how insufficient were all my pretensions to please a
> woman worthy of being pleased. (p.369)

Their conversation continues and Darcy, like his creator, now has to explain
why his behaviour was so inappropriate in the first place. Given the essentially non-existent knowledge of human neuro-psychology and neuro-
biology of the period, neither can provide sound reasons, so fall back on the
standard scapegoat of blaming the parents – particularly convenient in this
instance since the senior Mr and Mrs Darcy are dead so cannot speak up in
their own defence! Their son states that:

> As a child I was taught what was *right*, but I was not taught to correct
> my temper. I was given good principles, but left to follow them in
> pride and conceit. Unfortunately an only son, (for many years an
> only *child*) I was spoilt by my parents, who though good themselves,
> (my father particularly, all that was benevolent and amiable,)
> allowed, encouraged, almost taught me to be selfish and overbear-
> ing, to care for none beyond my own family circle, to think meanly
> of their sense and worth compared with my own. (p.369)

Although it is far from impossible to picture the sister of Lady Catherine
raising her son in such a manner, it is difficult to make this excuse fit with
everything else we have learned about the senior Mr Darcy. One can visualize him teaching his son the outward forms of his own good manners but
perhaps not realizing that the younger man was not absorbing the genuine
care and concern for others that was their underlying foundation. The
mother of a 22-year-old son is quoted as saying that his 'perception of reality is so different that when I hear him talk about his childhood, I swear we
must have lived in two different houses' (Barnhill 2002, p.207). Also, given
that they may have been in ill health for some time before dying, the Darcys
may not have had extensive opportunities to observe their son among
strangers, where his subtle difficulties are most noticeable. They, like their
devoted housekeeper, saw him mostly in familiar settings, where he was a
kind elder brother and a respectful, well-behaved and obedient son. Unlike
modern parents they would rarely have had opportunities to see him with
large groups of his peers at any age partly because, by the social norms of
their time, there were few about. As the principal landowners of the area

they 'did not visit' (p.265) with the inhabitants of the local village of Lambton.

This simplistic temptation to blame the parents appeared almost as soon as did the recognition of autism itself, beginning when Kanner may have confused cause and effect by noting signs of less attachment between parents and their autistic children, and not realizing that part of this may have been due to the lack of emotional reciprocity from the children. The 'refrigerator mother' hypothesis was a cruel and now discounted one. Infamously, it was Bruno Bettelheim who, 'primarily in the 1950s and 1960s, popularized the idea that autism was caused by maternal coldness toward their children – ignoring amongst other things, as Kanner did as well, that these same mothers had other children who were not autistic' (Laidler 2004, p.1).

As their analysis of their relationship thus far continues, Elizabeth probes further for reasons as to why Darcy fell in love with her. She speaks for him as she commands:

> 'Now be sincere; did you admire me for my impertinence?'
> 'For the liveliness of your mind, I did.'
> 'You may as well call it impertinence at once.' (p.380)

However, if impertinence and teasing are what Darcy finds attractive, he should already have fallen hard for Miss Caroline Bingley, who had been practising both strategies at closer quarters for much longer. Even now, Lizzy is still influencing our beliefs about Darcy by choosing words and motives for him that subtly emphasize a pride that needs puncturing. She does not seem to hear Darcy's quiet interjection about how he, like many men on the spectrum, was attracted by her lively mind and her intelligence.

Elizabeth continues in this way when discussing why Darcy appeared so haughty, unwilling to dance and uninterested in female company at the balls. Although being playful and witty, she again relies on her pride in her own perceptiveness about people as she overstates a possibility to him that:

> The fact is, that you were sick of civility, of deference, of officious attention. You were disgusted with the women who were always speaking and looking, and thinking for *your* approbation alone. I roused, and interested you, because I was so unlike *them*. Had you not been really amiable you would have hated me for it; but in spite of the pains you took to disguise yourself, your feelings were always noble and just; and in your heart, you thoroughly despised the persons who so assiduously courted you. There – I have saved you the

> trouble of accounting for it; and really, all things considered, I begin
> to think it perfectly reasonable. (p.380)

'Perfectly reasonable' and saves us all 'the trouble of accounting for it', so both the author and many critics since have been content with this explanation of his behaviour as *fact*. But notice that this is Lizzy's *opinion* only, and she has been wrong about men, and particularly about Darcy, before. Mr Darcy 'never explicitly agrees with or validates this account of his own motives' (Gilman 2000, p.227). We do not hear from his lips at this time that he despised or even noticed the women who had doubtless tried to capture his handsome person and equally handsome property. Many months earlier, in a conversation at Netherfield that included the Bingley sisters, he had made reference to 'there being a meanness in *all* the arts which ladies sometimes condescend to employ for captivation. Whatever bears affinity to cunning is despicable' (p.40). This comment reveals his strong preference for straightforward, unambiguous and honest dealings between people. However, he did not accuse all women of such stratagems. Also, although not as indiscriminately positive as Bingley, who declared that all young ladies qualify for the approbation, he spoke of knowing 'half a dozen...that are really accomplished' (p.39) even by his high standards, which included a well-rounded education, grace of manner and movement plus 'the improvement of her mind by extensive reading'(p.39). Ironically, readers often miss the fact that Darcy was not as negative about her fellow females as was Elizabeth who, in contrast to the six he believed he had met, proclaimed that she 'never saw such a woman [with]...such capacity, and taste, and application, and elegance, as you describe, united' (p.40).

In contrast to Elizabeth's attempt to explain Darcy, these pages have offered an alternative regarding his memorable and controversial behaviour the first time we meet him and he meets her. It and much else is accounted for if we realize and accept that he is at the mild end of the autistic spectrum.

Elizabeth, however, does not have the benefit of our modern knowledge in this field so her intense curiosity and keen intelligence drive her to keep questioning Darcy about his behaviour in various situations. As she stated months earlier at the dance at Netherfield, she wants to solve the puzzle of his personality:

> 'and I shall begin directly by asking you what made you so unwilling to come to the point at last. What made you so shy of me, when you first called, and afterwards dined here? Why, especially, when you called, did you look as if you did not care about me?'

'Because you were grave and silent, and gave me no encouragement.'

'But I was embarrassed.'

'And so was I.'

'You might have talked to me more when you came to dinner.'

'A man who had felt less, might.'

'... But I wonder how long you *would* have gone on, if you had
been left to yourself. I wonder when you *would* have spoken, if I had
not asked you!' (p.381)

Although Darcy assures her that he would have spoken again about his feelings for her and that he 'was not in a humour to wait for any opening of
your's...I was determined at once to know everything' (p.381), this may
indicate a slight lack of self-awareness as to how rarely and slowly he does
initiate conversation.

Although Elizabeth says she wonders *when* not *if* he would have proposed had she not taken the initiative, she will never know with absolute
certainty...and neither will we. This is one tiny piece of the puzzle that is
Fitzwilliam Darcy that will remain forever unsolved.

Part Four

Conclusion

12

Happily Ever After?

And then they all lived happily ever after. Or did they?

First and foremost, two centuries ago life itself was significantly more tenuous, so survival was the key issue with the 'happily' part a bonus rather than the expected outcome as it is today. In her book *The Gentleman's Daughter*, Amanda Vickery notes that:

> Recent revisionism may stress that the average woman ran only a 6–7 per cent risk of dying in her reproductive career, and was as likely to die by infectious disease or accident, but such statistics do not justify the claim that childbirth was seen as an insignificant cause of death. Even by the most revised figures, perinatal complication was probably the single most common cause of death in women aged twenty-five to thirty-four, accounting for one in five of all deaths in this age group…in a large village a woman might see a contemporary die in childbed every third year. (1998, p.97–8)

Still, given that Charlotte, Lydia and Elizabeth are healthy young women whose mothers survived numerous childbirths, the likelihood is that they will also. If the 'lived' part of the phrase is assumed what then about the 'happily'?

Those who erroneously dismiss Jane Austen's work as eighteenth-century chick-lit have critiqued the fact that each book ends around the time of the heroine's first kiss and/or wedding day (which, once upon a time, closely coincided). Little information is provided by the author about the later life of the people in the matches she created. Numerous sequels and even more informal speculation have attempted to fill in the future years she did not delineate.

Given the theories that I have proposed in this book, how would the autistic traits that five of these married characters possess influence their chances of marital bliss?

Mr and Mrs Bennet

With Mr and Mrs Bennet we have already read of the results of approximately 25 years of marriage between a couple who are both on the spectrum. The fruit of their union has been blighted by the progenitors themselves. Two of their daughters are on the autistic spectrum but all five have suffered from their parents' difficulties in putting their children's needs first...or even recognizing that these needs exist. As I described earlier, Jane, Elizabeth, Mary, Kitty and Lydia have, to varying degrees, experienced long-term verbal and emotional abuse as well as some physical neglect.

In her thought-provoking recent article, 'Asperger's Syndrome and Parenting', Sheila Jennings Linehan, a Toronto-based barrister and solicitor involved in family mediation, examines the roots of the potential difficulties involved when those with ASD are also parents. She writes, 'Parenting necessarily involves an intense interplay between parent and child cognition and between parent and child emotional reciprocity' (2004, p.1). She feels that 'Problems in parenting are linked directly to the core neuro-cognitive clinical features of Asperger's Syndrome itself, namely weak central coherence, poor cognitive shifting and lack of a theory of mind' (p.1). In particular this limited theory of mind, or 'mindblindness', is a concern as it 'in a mother is *the very opposite* of what we call "mothers' instinct"' (p.3). In addition to the many examples already described in their individual chapters, there is an instance early in the novel when both senior Bennets display what Linehan refers to when she notes that 'mindblind parents may have difficulty in distinguishing whether their child's actions are intentional or accidental...[which] adds enormous dysfunction to these families...[and] leads to very evident problems around child discipline, criticism, blame, and correcting behaviour with obvious related issues for child mental health' (p.3):

> Mrs Bennet...began scolding one of her daughters.
>
> 'Don't keep coughing so, Kitty, for heaven's sake! Have a little compassion on my nerves. You tear them to pieces.'
>
> 'Kitty has no discretion in her coughs,' said her father; 'she times them ill.'
>
> 'I do not cough for my own amusement,' replied Kitty fretfully. (p.6)

Imagine the effect on a child of hundreds of similar experiences of being blamed or misunderstood throughout his or her formative years. Mr Bennet has one more remark to make after delighting his family by telling them that he has called on the wealthy young Mr Bingley after all:

> 'Now, Kitty, you may cough as much as you chuse,' said Mr Bennet; and, as he spoke, he left the room, fatigued with the raptures of his wife. (p.8)

Mr Bennet's withdrawal from the family circle doubtless also happened a multitude of times during his daughters' growing years since, as Jennings Linehan notes, 'on the matter of sensory issues, these parents frequently attest that they find it difficult to tolerate the normal noise, mess and chaos of childhood' (p.2) and family life.

With only Mary left at home the Bennets' negative impact on their daughters' well-being will be markedly lessened, although the emotional effects and painful, puzzling memories will linger throughout their lives.

The Bennets' marriage will continue on much as it has, with the improvement, as previously noted, that Mrs Bennet will be significantly less anxious now that two daughters have acquired husbands wealthy enough to support her and her other daughters if necessary. As in the past, she will draw any emotional and social support she needs not from her husband but from her siblings, Mrs Philips and Mr Gardiner, and from the women of her neighbourhood. As for Mr Bennet, he will continue avoiding such social encounters when possible by retreating to either his own library or the well-maintained one at Pemberley. Fortunately, neither Bennet is likely to seek or have a central role in raising the next generation.

Mr and Mrs Wickham

Ah! The Wickhams.

They could be voted the couple least likely to celebrate their fiftieth wedding anniversary, or even their fifth! However, they will wildly join in any excuse for a celebration in the years they do have together. Estimating how many that will be, or even if they will be counted in months not years, depends on the optimistic or pessimistic nature of the amateur actuary. Certainly Elizabeth, one of the first to speculate on their potential for wedded bliss, is not hopeful. As she confronts the irony of being relieved about the wedding while at the same time nervous about the marriage, she cries out to Jane:

> How strange this is! And for *this* we are to be thankful. That they
> should marry, small as is their chance of happiness, and wretched as
> is his character, we are forced to rejoice! Oh, Lydia! (p.304)

The charming but morally wretched Wickham does not strike us as someone who will make old bones. Austen does tell us that 'his affection for [his
wife] soon sank into indifference' (p.387) and that Lydia occasionally visits
Pemberley 'when her husband was gone to enjoy himself in London or
Bath' (p.387), where it does not require much elasticity of imagination to
picture him shot in a duel or breaking his neck leaping out a window pur-
sued by an irate husband or merchant. Historically, the 'restoration of peace'
(p.387) decreased the possibility that his death might have occurred while
honourably serving his country rather than dishonourably servicing a
matron or maid.

Lydia is protected from worrying about her future (or lack of it with
such an unreliable husband) by her attention deficit hyperactivity disorder
issues, which render her impulsive and distractable so she lives totally in the
fleeting, ever-changing present. Her ADHD is probably a large component
of why she chose such a mate in the first place. Ratey and Johnson, in *Shadow
Syndromes*, describe a Lydia clone when they say that, in a woman, 'her
ADD-ish energy levels and enthusiasm can give her a high-voltage appeal'
and that 'she may actually select *for* trouble in her choice of mate…[so] her
tremendous need for stimulation can reap a whirlwind' (1997, p.190).

If the marriage does last, Lydia's autistic tendencies will render her
oblivious both to the faults of her husband and also to the reactions those
faults provoke in others. Even if 'Bingley's good humour was overcome' by
their overlong visits it will not really be an effective way to clear his home of
the Wickhams if he only 'proceeded so far as to *talk* of giving them a hint to
be gone' (p.387). This is a couple who will be oblivious to a mere hint and
will require a much blunter heave-ho to propel them out of the exasperated
host's door.

Of course, our concern for the future of their marriage is not primarily
due to the senior Wickhams but rather any little juniors who bounce out
into the world. Not for them a soft landing into a cradle of painstakingly
hand-sewn linen as their young, ADHD mother, like some others with that
diagnosis, is 'flamboyant, energetic, and an enormous amount of fun, but
completely irresponsible and unable to see any project through to its end'
(p.183). Figuratively at least, a wee Wickham's infancy may well resemble
that of the poor babe tumbling from its gin-drunk mother's lap in Hogarth's

famous image. Those that manage to survive will be left to scramble for themselves as they lead an unpredictable life with a madcap mother who swoops them up in her arms one minute and forgets to see to their basic needs the next. They may be children who will ultimately find solace and a safe refuge with their Aunt and Uncle Bingley; however, the ones who resemble their mother neurologically may well become bored with that worthy pair and rocket back to their parents' less predictable but livelier lifestyle.

Mr and Mrs Collins

Although, when she first hears of the forthcoming marriage of this couple, Elizabeth declares it to be 'impossible' (p.124), it does occur and, indeed, is approaching its first anniversary by the time her own venture into married life takes place. Rarely has a bride entered into marriage with her eyes so clearly open, taking not the slightest rosy glance through tinted glasses. Charlotte's decision to accept Mr Collins was motivated 'solely from the pure and disinterested desire of an establishment' (p.122) as marriage was:

> the only honourable provision for well-educated young women of small fortune, and however uncertain of giving happiness, must be their pleasantest preservative from want. This preservative she had now obtained; and at the age of twenty-seven, without having ever been handsome, she felt all the good luck of it. (p.123)

Charlotte knows that she has secured a financially stable future for herself and for any children she may have, as Mr Collins can both offer a home and income now and the promise of even finer ones in the future when he inherits Longbourn. Fortunately, given his interpersonal ineptness, in order to retain his current employment, Mr Collins has only to please Lady Catherine not an entire congregation or a Ministry and Personnel Committee. Even his tendency to monologue becomes socially acceptable when he dons his robes and speaks from the pulpit!

In our century Charlotte would have other options besides marriage to secure her financial future. Therefore, she would have expected additional benefits before entering a marital relationship. Indeed, according to Aston this may be 'why more men with Asperger syndrome are being identified today'. As she notes:

> With the rise in number of jobs available to women and the increase
> in women's capacity to earn, the traditional dependence on a man as
> the sole financial supporter, has, for some women, decreased. As
> women become more independent, they ask for support in more
> areas than just the financial side of the relationship. Most women
> want more from their partners than just money... Thus the numbers
> of men with Asperger syndrome may simply have increased because
> their problems with social interaction are no longer being sidelined.
> (2001, p.17)

Fewer women (or their families) nowadays would have to take the one-
dimensional view of Mr Collins that Charlotte does and be content simply
because he is earning an income.

Beyond meeting her own need for financial security, Charlotte has the
additional gratification of knowing that her marriage is a source of delight
and relief for her parents and siblings. Indeed, her:

> whole family in short were properly overjoyed on the occasion. The
> younger girls formed hopes of *coming out* a year or two sooner than
> they might otherwise have done; and the boys were relieved from
> their apprehension of Charlotte's dying an old maid. (p.122)

By accepting Mr Collins she has benefited her entire family as her parents
are relieved of the need to support her in the present and her brothers of a
similar responsibility in the future. Unlike the Bennet family, hers seems to
have held to the social norm of trying to avoid having younger daughters
enter the marital market until the eldest daughter had been taken off it. Her
delay in finding a husband was yearly increasing the likelihood that her sisters would not marry either. This had significant implications for the entire
family's well-being.

Although Charlotte knows that everyone else, including the prospective groom, is pleased by her decision, she is painfully aware that the 'least
agreeable circumstance in the business, was the surprise it must occasion to
Elizabeth Bennet, whose friendship she valued beyond that of any other
person' (p.123). Despite Lizzy's astonished reaction Charlotte remains calm
as she rationally explains her expectations of marriage in general and hers in
particular:

> I am not romantic you know. I never was. I ask only a comfortable
> home; and considering Mr Collins's character, connections, and sit-
> uation in life, I am convinced that my chance of happiness with him

is as fair, as most people can boast on entering the marriage state.
(p.125)

Given her limited aims she is not as likely to experience disappointment as are those whose lofty expectations include being continually happy, never feeling lonely and always being 'as one' with their partner.

Charlotte hopes only for a home and physically she has one. How could this house not be ideal when even the very shelves in its closets have been decreed by the exalted Lady Catherine De Bourgh? The frequent presence of this doyenne of dictatorial decorators is one of the two potential, indeed perpetual, irritations in the 'comfortable home' Charlotte has obtained. As any urban dweller knows, in real estate the mantra is 'location, location, location'. It is not just the house but the neighbourhood and ultimately the neighbours in the 'hood who determine the pleasure of residence. In this case the Collinses have all the benefits and burdens of 'a most attentive neighbour' (p.157), complete with carriages but also with condescension and unceasing comments about every aspect of their lives, from the arrangement of their furniture to the 'too large' (p.169) joints of meat that they serve. Regrettably, they are short of alternatives as their contact with others in the locale is limited due to the fact that 'the style of living of the neighbourhood in general, was beyond the Collinses' reach' (p.169).

So, physically, while Charlotte's much desired home is 'rather small, but well built and convenient' (p.157), the selection of companions with whom she can build a truly close and caring bond is even smaller. Unfortunately, neither is there anyone *within* the house with whom such a relationship is possible. Charlotte might have been better served if she had been able to marry a naval man or someone else whose profession took him away often as, in modern parlance, marrying Mr Collins is very much a 24/7 commitment. In order not to have her husband and his monologues constantly with her, Charlotte has devised such strategies as selecting a small, viewless room at the back of the house for her sitting room and encouraging her spouse to engage in gardening supposedly for 'the healthfulness of the exercise' (p.156). Both his physical and her mental health no doubt benefit from his horticultural exertions.

However, it is their relationship not just in their house but in their *bedroom* that both fascinates and repulses the modern reader. As Ruth Perry wrote in her article 'Sleeping with Mr Collins', 'the physical repugnance that we in the present century feel at the idea of sleeping with Mr Collins is entirely absent in Jane Austen's treatment of the matter' (2000, p.2). She explains that:

> The reason that Austen is able to imagine Charlotte's sleeping with Mr Collins with equanimity is because sex had less psychological significance in eighteenth-century England than in our own post-Freudian era; it was less tied to individual identity, and more understood as an uncomplicated, straightforward physical appetite. Sexual disgust – the feeling that sex with the 'wrong' person could be viscerally disturbing – was an invention of the eighteenth century. (p.5)

The fact that Charlotte can state that she is 'not romantic' (p.125) means that she can accept the physical aspect of their marriage as precisely that: physical not emotional. She can rejoice in the arrival of their 'young olive branch' (p.364) without expending angst as to how he or she was planted:

> The resigned attitude which leads Charlotte to marry Collins also makes it possible for her to live with him with far less pain than Elizabeth would experience in a like situation. She takes the same cold-blooded and practical attitude toward keeping Collins at a distance that she had taken earlier in encouraging his advances. During her visit to Hunsford, Elizabeth is compelled to appreciate Charlotte's 'address in guiding, and composure in bearing with her husband, and to acknowledge that it was done very well' (II, v). We are left with the feeling, however, that Charlotte has committed herself to a barren existence by which she is bound, eventually, to feel oppressed. (Paris 1978, p.114)

Besides predicting that Charlotte will find that she has a 'barren existence', Paris also wonders if 'she will be forced, in time, to adopt the defensive irony of a Mr Bennet' (1978, p.114).

First of all, to use an alternative meaning for the homonym 'barren', Charlotte's life will soon be quite the opposite as it will centre around her soon-to-be-born child and any further possible offshoots of her marital relations with her husband. The joys and concerns of motherhood will fill to overflowing the routine of her days. As the eldest of a large and lively family she knew and presumably desired the realities of life with children when she entered into marriage.

Second, as I have shown, Mr Bennet's defensive ironies, or lack of empathy towards others, arise as much from his neurological make-up as from his life situation. Charlotte is not a self-centred individual like him, hence she will be able to view any situation in her marriage from her husband's perspective as well as her own. Therefore, she will be unlikely to fall into such cruel negativity. When Mr Bennet married he was probably so focused on his prospective wife's body that he did not see past it to her personality. In complete contrast Charlotte has a clear, unromantic view of her spouse's strengths and weaknesses right from the start. Her low expectations mean she will not be disappointed or feel robbed. Also her practical, unimaginative nature may well protect her from the depression and stress that befall so many unknowingly married to a partner on the autistic spectrum.

Finally, although some dismiss Mr Collins as 'clearly ineducable' (Emsley 2005, p.86), there is hope for small, incremental improvements in his social graces. He is still a young man in his mid-twenties and, for the first time in his life, the primary influence on him will come from someone who is perceptive about others. Neither his early life with his miserly, withdrawn father nor his present life under the domination of Lady Catherine have provided him with appropriate guidance or models. Charlotte's growing awareness of how to curb his excessively formal and fawning manners is shown when she pre-arranges to have the responsibility of introducing her father, sister and friend to Lady Catherine. As an intelligent woman she will continue to guide him, but will do so in a subtle manner. Already Mr Collins believes that they have 'but one mind and one way of thinking' (p.216), and his practical, astute wife will endeavour to keep him believing that while at the same time hers becomes the mind that steers their path through life.

Once Mr Collins inherits Mr Bennet's property, he will be removed from Lady Catherine's overpowering influence. Talking to or about her brings out the worst of his autistic traits so distance from her will be therapeutic. As mistress of Longbourn, Charlotte will further benefit by having a larger home and income, as well as companionship among those in the community in which she grew up. Her parents may still be alive and, if not, a brother and his family will have inherited their house. Besides contact with relatives her broader social circle will expand since the Collinses will be the possessors of one of the principal properties in the area. The fact that he will be a landowner will give Mr Collins significant status, which will help balance his somewhat odd behaviours. Eventually, as is the way in small communities, people will get used to him and accept his idiosyncrasies as 'just the way he is'. With a farm and workers to supervise rather than merely a

172 / SO ODD A MIXTURE

garden to keep him out of doors, Mr Collins will have much to occupy him, hence he will be even less often at his wife's side during the day. With his attention to detail and interest in growing things, Mr Collins may even generate more income from the land he inherits than does his predecessor who takes so little interest in it.

The children they may have will benefit from the good sense and order of a home life directed by their mother as well as from the good humour and sociability of their mother's family. The affable Sir William will be a loving grandfather; it is a delight to picture him dancing with a small granddaughter in his arms or listening attentively to the confidences of a young grandson. Having observed the poor example of the previous owners of Longbourn, Charlotte will make sure that money is set aside annually to provide for the future of any other children she and her spouse have besides the first-born male. Although she will actually manage their family life Charlotte will continue to treat her husband with respect so not hold him up to ridicule in front of their children.

The other details of his relationship to his little ones are somewhat harder to predict. As Attwood has noted, there 'is a difficulty for the person with Asperger's syndrome, if they're a parent, understanding natural childhood abilities and behaviour...[so they often] don't know how to relate to their kids' (2000, p.26). Given that the Collins family inhabit a smaller home with fewer servants than the Darcy family at Pemberley, Mr Collins will have less choice about how much contact he has with his offspring. If his sensory system is overwhelmed by them he may frequently need to retreat to his bees or to books as did Mr Bennet before him. On the other hand, Mr Collins may be led by his children to grow emotionally. Having been raised by an isolated, undemonstrative father with no one else to offer him affection, Mr Collins may respond very positively, if at first awkwardly, to the smiles, trust and love offered so winningly by his infants and toddlers.

As the novel ends, both Mr and Mrs Collins have achieved the specific if limited goals they desired from marriage; therefore, basking in this small, warm glow of success, they do not feel bitterness or resentment towards each other. They are content and treat each other pleasantly. 'Elizabeth gradually realized, once over the first shock of horror, that her friend was after all making a tolerable life for herself in the second-best world that most people except heroines have to inhabit' (Harding 1968, p.99). As Elizabeth leaves Hunsford she feels sorry for her friend 'to leave her to such society' (p.216), but notes that, 'Her home and her housekeeping, her parish and her poultry, and all their dependent concerns, had not yet lost their charms' (p.216). Perhaps they never will.

As he farewells his cousin, Mr Collins refers to his 'dear Charlotte' and adds, 'Only let me assure you, my dear Miss Elizabeth, that I can from my heart most cordially wish you equal felicity in marriage' (p.216).

Mr and Mrs Darcy

Miss Elizabeth Bennet and Mr Fitwilliam Darcy are preceded into marriage by the senior Bennets, the Wickhams and the Collinses, three other couples who, like them, have ASD as part of what at least one partner brings to the marital mix. Good wishes for their union include Mr Collins's hope that they have 'equal felicity in marriage' (p.216) to him and his bride, as well as Lydia's exuberant prediction that if her sister loves 'Mr Darcy half as well as I do my dear Wickham [she] must be very happy' (p.386). The longer-wed Mrs Bennet disregards these fripperies of emotion in order to focus on the material aspect. Therefore she is also convinced that her daughter will have every reason to be happy as she trumpets in delight:

> Oh! My sweetest Lizzy! How rich and how great you will be! What pin-money, what jewels, what carriages you will have!... A house in town! Everything that is charming!... Ten thousand a year! (p.378)

Mrs Bennet is right about these factual aspects, but are Mr Collins and Lydia correct as well? Will Elizabeth be happy? Will Darcy? Many, many people including romantic teenagers, bright graduate students, ambitious academics and nostalgic grandparents have speculated in private or in print on these very questions. Most have been very optimistic, including Sarah Emsley, who believes that this 'marriage will be a marriage of equals' (2005, p.102) as they have each helped their loved one to overcome 'their tendency to judge others before they judge themselves' (p.95). However, Sarah Arthur, even though her *Dating Mr Darcy* holds him up as 'the ideal' (2005, p.x) and encourages young women to find a partner with similar qualities of integrity and intelligence, expresses some concern that:

> If their first few encounters are any indication, Lizzy and Darcy will have some interesting communication issues to work out once they finally get together. For starters, their relationship begins with verbal sparring – not the best of habits to form at the beginning of a lifelong partnership! (p.44)

Communication issues are indeed central in any marriage, even those not complicated by the presence of some symptoms of an autistic spectrum disorder. The key factor, however, is that Lizzy, like most brides of our century and the one past, enters marriage with high expectations hence the bar for success/happiness in her case is precariously set at a somewhat less attainable level than it is for the practical Charlotte or the thoughtless Lydia.

Over the last few centuries the characteristics that increase the likelihood of a happy, solid marriage have been the subject of hundreds of books and thousands upon thousands of hours of thought. From this collective wisdom four frequently mentioned key areas will be examined in relation to the union of Fitzwilliam Darcy and Elizabeth Bennet. These are:

1.   economic resources

2.   social supports

3.   personality traits

4.   that great intangible, love.

The last shall be dealt with first.

Love, love, love

One of the chief prognostic concerns is the foundation and quality of Elizabeth's feelings for Mr Darcy. Does she or doesn't she? Does she love him or does she, like Charlotte, primarily marry to obtain a house?

As Paris notes, for the greater part of the novel, '[t]he major obstacle to the marriage is, of course, Elizabeth's dislike of Darcy' (1978, p.99). He feels that the creation, overcoming and ultimate destroying of this obstacle drives the plot since 'the central action of the novel is the evolution of that dislike, its gradual softening after Darcy's first proposal, and the emergence of Elizabeth's desire for the marriage during her visit to Pemberley' (p.99). Paris feels that Lizzy's original dislike is created by the severe blow to her pride when Darcy refuses to dance with her and dismisses her as 'tolerable' (p.12) the first time they meet. Although his 'letter clears away many of Elizabeth's objections to his character…[i]t does not arouse, however, a desire for his attentions or regret for her decision' (p.130). The letter, in other words, shifts her feelings from dislike to neutrality. The move to more positive emotions, in Paris's opinion, occurs only when '[t]he magnificence of Pemberley not only wins Elizabeth's admiration, it also feeds her pride' (p.130). He feels that, '[i]f, before, Elizabeth was disposed to think ill of

Darcy because he had hurt her pride, she is now disposed to think well of him because he has fed it' (p.131). The beauty of the grounds and 'the grandeur of the house bring home to Elizabeth the magnitude of Darcy's proposal' (p.130). Paris feels that Elizabeth is flattered by Darcy and believes that his continuing affection for her, despite all the obstacles of which he was initially so well aware, confirms that 'she *is*, after all, a superior being...a woman whose personal worth is so great as to compensate for the undesirability of her connections' (p.134).

Paris bases much of his analysis on Lizzy's much-quoted statement that her love began 'from my first seeing his beautiful grounds at Pemberley' (p.378). Paris acknowledges that she is joking while saying this, but points out that 'things said in jest often reveal the deepest truths: and our understanding of Elizabeth's character gives us good reason to take her answer seriously' (1978, p.130).

However, the one who knows Lizzy longest and best does not take it seriously. This laughing reference to the grounds of Pemberley takes place at the beginning of 'half the night spent in conversation' (p.374) with her beloved sister, Jane, who, although she tends to trust everyone, is originally 'absolutely incredulous' (p.372) about the news of Lizzy's engagement to Darcy. She repeatedly questions first its very existence and then its motivation:

'And do you really love him quite well enough? Oh, Lizzy! do anything rather than marry without affection. Are you quite sure that you feel what you ought to do?'

'Oh, yes! You will only think I feel *more* than I ought to do, when I tell you all.'

'What do you mean?'

'Why, I must confess, that I love him better than I do Bingley. I am afraid that you will be angry.'

'My dearest sister, now *be* serious. I want to talk very seriously. Let me know every thing that I am to know, without delay. Will you tell me how long you have loved him?'

'It has been coming on so gradually, that I hardly know when it began. But I believe I must date it from my first seeing his beautiful grounds at Pemberley.'

Another entreaty that she would be serious, however, produced the desired effect; and she soon satisfied Jane by her solemn assur-

ances of attachment. When convinced on that article, Miss Bennet
had nothing farther to wish. (pp.372–3)

The jocular reference to Pemberley occurs in the same style as Lizzy's teasing pretence that gentle Jane will be 'angry' at her for loving Darcy more
than Bingley. Neither comment is created or credited as a serious one.

Jane does not for a moment think that this reference to Pemberley
reveals a genuine motive but she is ultimately convinced by 'her solemn
assurances of attachment' (p.373) that her sister's love for Darcy is real. Nor
is there any reason for us to believe otherwise if we look back at Lizzy's
thoughts when she first saw those beautiful grounds. Naturally, as we would
be, Elizabeth was struck by the true elegance and good taste of the property
and its situation. She was momentarily stunned by the dreamlike realization
that, had she accepted Darcy, this would have been the home to which she
could have welcomed those she loved, such as her aunt and uncle:

> 'But no,' – recollecting herself, – 'that could never be: my uncle and
> aunt would have been lost to me: I should not have been allowed to
> invite them.'
>
> This was a lucky recollection – it saved her from something like
> regret. (p.246)

Her relationships to those she loves take precedence instantly over real
estate, no matter how desirable.

Elizabeth's opinion of Darcy starts to shift not due to his house but to
his housekeeper. The praise of him offered by Mrs Reynolds was 'most
opposite to her ideas' (p.248), but she is flexible enough in her thought pro-
cesses to be open to new information and to reconsider her theories. 'Elizabeth listened, wondered, doubted and was impatient for more' (p.249).
Then she stands in 'earnest contemplation' (p.250) before his portrait
wherein the artist has captured him in his home looking relaxed and
smiling:

> There was certainly at this moment, in Elizabeth's mind, a more
> gentle sensation towards the original, than she had ever felt at the
> height of their acquaintance. The commendation bestowed on him
> by Mrs Reynolds was of no trifling nature. What praise is more valu-
> able than the praise of an intelligent servant? As a brother, a
> landlord, a master, she considered how many people's happiness
> were in his guardianship! – How much of pleasure or pain it was in
> his power to bestow! – How much of good and evil must be done by

him! Every idea that had been brought forward by the housekeeper was favourable to his character, and as she stood before the canvas, on which he was represented, and fixed his eyes upon herself, she thought of his regard with a deeper sentiment of gratitude than it had ever raised before; she remembered its warmth, and softened its impropriety of expression. (p.251)

Elizabeth is starting to consider Darcy in a more positive manner, not because of his wealth but because of how well he, although still a young man, is handling the responsibility of it. 'She considered how many people's happiness were in his guardianship' (p.251). Unlike many a young rake of that period or similar youth featured in our current entertainment periodicals, Darcy is not wasting his time, health and inheritance by gambling or with addictions of other sorts. On a whim he could negatively alter the lives and livelihoods of his tenants, servants and sister. He has not; all who are dependent on him 'give him a good name' (p.249). How different is his reputation among those who know him long and well than it was among those whose judgements were based on a fleeting acquaintance.

Her experiences as a daughter have already given Elizabeth vivid and deeply painful examples as to how the vulnerable are affected when the man in the family shirks the responsibilities of his role. As she has matured in the course of this eventful year she has begun to recognize that marriage, although a personal union, also has an immense impact on the wider social/familial sphere. Donne's phrase that no man is an island is doubly true of a couple:

Elizabeth has a regard for the social aspects of marriage, but she seems to represent at the outset a predominantly individualistic point of view. Her change of heart toward Darcy is profoundly influenced, however, by social considerations... Mrs Reynolds' description of his exemplary behavior in his many social roles impresses Elizabeth quite as much as the information that he has a good temper. *Elizabeth's experiences with her father have prepared her to appreciate such evidence of responsibility.* When we consider that she finds herself drawn to the idea of being Darcy's wife before her renewed contact with the man himself, we must conclude that Darcy's social attractiveness plays a large part in the awakening of her desire. (Paris 1978, p.105, my italics)

That this short visit to Pemberley has initiated a profound shift in Elizabeth's attitude to Darcy is, in my opinion, due to what she has learned about him as a person not what she has seen of his property. To these second-hand opinions she now has a totally unsought opportunity to add to her own first-hand knowledge when Darcy unexpectedly returns to his home a day early in advance of his invited guests.

Darcy's behaviour to this surprising trio of uninvited guests is exemplary. His civility to Lizzy's beloved uncle and aunt shows her that the positive descriptions of him she has been hearing certainly are true in this setting. As Darcy himself later tells her, his desire 'was to shew you, by every civility in my power, that I was not so mean as to resent the past; and I hoped to obtain your forgiveness, to lessen your ill opinion, by letting you see that your reproofs had been attended to' (p.370).

Darcy's attentive behaviour both then and when he brings his sister and Bingley to visit her at the inn in Lambton adds to Elizabeth's mental and emotional confusion about him. Her thoughts and feelings are so unsettled that 'she lay awake two whole hours, endeavouring to make them out' (p.265). The conclusions she reaches are that:

- 'She certainly did not hate him' (p.265)

- she felt 'respect created by the conviction of his valuable qualities' (p.265)

- above all, she felt 'Gratitude, not merely for having once loved her, but for loving her still well enough, to forgive all the petulance and acrimony of her manner in rejecting him, and all the unjust accusations accompanying her rejection' (p.265).

If 'gratitude and esteem are good foundations of affection' (p.279) and provide the nurturing soil for a relationship, then love radiating from the other is the sunshine. The fact that he still loves her is a powerful stimulant to the seeds of love newly planted within her. Love can create love.

Ironically, personifying the truth inherent in the old saying, 'you don't know what you've got 'til it's gone', Elizabeth only fully realizes that she would like to marry Darcy when she feels that the possibility no longer exists. Having Wickham added to her family surely precludes adding Darcy. After all, 'it was not to be supposed that Mr Darcy would connect himself with a family, where to every other objection would now be added, an alliance and relationship of the nearest kind with the man whom he so justly scorned' (p.311). The power of deciding for or against marriage no longer seems to be hers: 'She was convinced that she could have been happy with him; when it was no longer likely they should meet' (p.311). Having firmly told her first suitor that she was 'not one of those young ladies...who are so daring as to risk their happiness on the chance of being asked a second time' (p.107), Elizabeth now despairs that her second suitor will never re-voice that request which she now so desires. In agony:

> She began now to comprehend that he was exactly the man, who, in disposition and talents, would most suit her. His understanding and temper, though unlike her own, would have answered all her wishes. It was a union that must have been to the advantage of both; by her ease and liveliness, his mind might have been softened, his manners improved, and from his judgement, information, and knowledge of the world, she must have received benefit of great importance. (p.312)

Weeks later, Elizabeth's father, like her sister, initially does not believe that her intense dislike of Mr Darcy has changed into love. Mr Bennet probes as to whether Darcy's riches motivate her and refers to him as 'a proud, unpleasant sort of man' (p.376), which ironically is the belief that Lizzy's own delight in a humorous anecdote helped establish as fact in her family and local community. 'How earnestly did she then wish that her former opinions had been more reasonable, her expressions more moderate!' (p.376). Stung by her father's disbelief, and doubtless feeling embarrassed by her previous vehemence, Elizabeth tries to convince him of her change of attitude and heart towards Darcy:

> 'I do, I do like him,' she replied, with tears in her eyes, 'I love him. Indeed he has no improper pride. He is perfectly amiable. You do not know what he really is; then pray do not pain me by speaking of him in such terms.' (p.376)

Like his eldest daughter, her father, knowing even less of what has transpired during the past year, has difficulty adapting to such a dramatic change from Lizzy's first impressions. He advises her to 'think better of it' and warns her that her 'lively talents would place you in the greatest danger in an unequal marriage' (p.376).

> Elizabeth, still more affected, was earnest and solemn in her reply; and at length, by repeated assurances that Mr Darcy was really the object of her choice, by explaining the gradual change which her estimation of him had undergone, relating her absolute certainty that his affection was not the work of a day, but had stood the test of

many months suspense, and enumerating with energy all his good qualities, she did conquer her father's incredulity and reconcile him to the match. (p.377)

Would Elizabeth have been able to convince both her best beloved sister and her father of her deep and genuine love for Darcy if it was not real? Both were initially sceptical and not satisfied with her first statements. The two Bennets differ widely in their experiences, characters, perspectives and their attitudes towards love. One has found a compatible marriage partner and the other regrets not having done so. For both to be convinced, then, Elizabeth must have been expressing her deepest and truest feelings. Therefore, Lizzy loves Darcy.

That Darcy loves Elizabeth has not been questioned to any significant degree. Neither he himself nor his formidable aunt have been able to convince him otherwise. It is a feeling unexplainable in words alone. He has proven that his love can withstand many obvious barriers, including perceived social inequalities, challenging in-laws, humiliation, financial burdens and, most dauntingly, his beloved's initial and seemingly insurmountable rejection of him as 'the last man in the world whom I could ever be prevailed upon to marry' (p.193).

By the end of the novel their love for each other includes, but is not limited to, the physical/sexual attraction that two healthy, handsome people in their twenties bring to a union, as well as their respect for each other's capabilities, and gratitude on both of their parts: her gratitude for his selfless assistance to her family and his for how her insights have improved his character. And, of course, their love includes that unknowable certain something that can not fully be analysed by others or themselves.

The fact that their love is multi-faceted makes it stronger and more resilient. This is not a love at first sight or a delicate untried love, but one that has already had to survive many, many challenges. It has been tested and strengthened by time, distance and adversity:

> His love for Elizabeth makes him a better person, brings out the excellence of his character. Her dawning love for him gives depth to her character, gives her experience of more than just laughter at absurdity, awakens heretofore untouched reserves of gratitude, admiration, and tenderness... Elizabeth and Darcy have seen each other at their very worst, and they love each other anyway. (Sherrod 1989, pp.68–9)

So, Elizabeth loves Darcy and Darcy loves Elizabeth. No doubt they will have their intertwined initials carved over the doorways of any new buildings at Pemberley. However, do these two facts add up to the achievement of 'living happily ever after' when the two become one? What will protect or weaken their marriage during the 'for better and for worse' times that befall any relationship that lasts long enough? How will ASD impact their married life?

Economic resources

Ironically, Mrs Bennet's focus on Darcy's riches is a realistic acknowledgement of their powerful and positive role in the marriage. His wealth gives them the economic stability that, then as now, is one cornerstone when building a solid marital relationship. Arguments about how to allocate scarce resources and fears of bankruptcy worry and ultimately rot many a marriage. Money even makes easier the 'in sickness and in health' part of the wedding vows. Given the woman's major role as care giver in most families, any long-term illness that befalls her can impact harshly on her ability to care for a home and children, thus put enormous stress on the family unit, sometimes leading to its break-up as little ones are parcelled out to various relations. Married to a wealthy man with a competent housekeeper and numerous other servants, Lizzy will not have to worry about being physically able to care for her loved ones. In life we have at our disposal, to varying degrees, *time, energy* and *money;* any of these can be used to save the other two, but we cannot save all three at the same time. Mr and Mrs Darcy's ample financial resources mean they can spend money in order to have more time and energy for each other and for those whom they care about. The enormous and exhausting time pressure issues facing most dual-income-earning young couples of our century will not confront them.

However, fiscal concerns can certainly be an unusually dominant issue for modern families when one of the couple has an autistic spectrum disorder. Sometimes, fortunately, ASD is a real financial benefit for them if the individual's intense special interest is one to which our society assigns a high monetary value. Those with strengths in numerical or visual/spatial areas may earn excellent salaries in fields such as engineering, accounting or computer technology. Those who combine high intelligence with the ability to focus for long periods of time on very specific ideas may receive social and financial rewards for the research they conduct: 'It is here, in the autistic person's ability to seize and pursue one subject for a lifetime, that we see the connection between the terrible deficits of autism, and its terrible brilliance' (Ratey and Johnson 1997, p.273).

However, sometimes even seemingly mild ASD impacts negatively on the person's ability to earn a family-supporting wage. Even selecting a career or job path to pursue may be unexpectedly difficult for some otherwise capable individuals. Planning a career requires high-level executive functioning, which may not be present. This inability to reach a decision also seems to be associated with difficulty with imagination in that some literally cannot picture themselves in a particular position or profession. In contrast most people start off as children imagining themselves as ballet dancers, fire-fighters and veterinarians, then gradually refine these images into vocations that encompass their true abilities and interests.

Even those who can achieve a career may experience occupational difficulties in the interview process, which almost always involves meeting new people, as well as many subtle social nuances. Once a job is obtained social skills are usually essential to maintain it. In addition, for some people with ASD, the sensory issues of working in a crowded office may overwhelm them. Fluorescent lights, high levels of background noise and the modern pressure to multi-task are particularly debilitating for many.

Naturally, if there are significant problems with employment the stress on the marriage is high. A source of income is essential for any couple because money 'is at the core of all three of the universally defined human needs: food, shelter and clothing. They all cost money' (Stanford 2003, p.143).

It is fortunate indeed that Fitzwilliam Darcy has inherited a fortune! He will never have to go through a job interview, work cooperatively on a committee or please an employer. He did not even have to decide on a career, as his life's work was laid out before him from the moment he raised his head from the snugness of his cradle. He may have chosen a different bride than that intended for him then, but he has not rejected the highly enviable life of a wealthy English landowner.

Social supports

However, social impoverishment, not finances, is the concern raised by Darcy's aunt, who holds an extremely negative view for the future of a union between a Darcy and a Bennet. Her verbal rant to Elizabeth in the shrubbery includes concerns that:

- 'the shades of Pemberley [are] to be thus polluted' (p.357)

- 'a connection with you must disgrace him in the eyes of everybody' (p.357)

- '[you are] determined to ruin him in the opinion of all his friends, and make him the contempt of the world' (p.358).

All Lady Catherine's thoughts are around the social or public view of the marriage; none considers the personal or private happiness of the pair.

Elizabeth counters these objections to their marriage with the statement that they do come from the same broad social sphere in that 'He is a gentleman; I am a gentleman's daughter; so far we are equal' (p.356). Lady Catherine unwillingly agrees: 'True. You *are* a gentleman's daughter,' but counters with, 'But who was your mother? Who are your uncles and aunts?' (p.356). As a member of an older generation Lady Catherine puts far more emphasis on *rank* than she does on *class* or income. As explained by Thomas Keymer in his essay in *Jane Austen in Context*:

> Where 'class' would be measured in terms above all of productivity and income, locating individuals in socio-economic positions attained through material success, 'rank' placed primary emphasis on lineage, implying that social status was more or less inalienably conferred by birth and descent. (2005, p.387)

However, Lady Catherine's belief that those high in rank will automatically disassociate themselves from the Darcys shows her disconnection from the changes in the England of that period: 'Jane Austen wrote, and was published, in a period of profound economic transition in Great Britain, characterised by revolutions agricultural and industrial' (Keymer 2005, p.415). Although the gentry stigmatized trade on the one hand they offered their other hand in marriage to the daughters and granddaughters of the traders in order to attach those fortunes to their lands and pay for improvements to their grandiose houses. We are not the first generation to overspend on renovations. Similarly, the male descendants of those businessmen infiltrated the gentry as they became owners of country homes of their own.

That such distinctions of rank were not as important to him as to his aunt had already been shown by Darcy's choosing as his closest friend, Charles Bingley, a young man who 'inherited property to the amount of nearly an hundred thousand pounds from his father' (p.15), whose fortune 'had been acquired by trade' (p.15). Also, someone as uncomfortable in large groups as Mr Darcy is not likely to seek out those settings where 'the eyes of everybody', to which his aunt referred, will be fixed upon him.

Socially, therefore, the Darcys will not be ostracized by those with whom they would like to associate; neither has a desire to make a splash in the larger social pond, but rather craves 'the comfort and elegance of their family party at Pemberley' (p.384). In that setting they are assured of strong bonds of caring and social support.

Each brings full or partial responsibility for a younger sister into this family party they are creating. With respect to *his* Georgiana, 'the attachment of the sisters was exactly what Darcy had hoped to see. They were able to love each other, even as well as they intended. Georgiana had the highest opinion in the world of Elizabeth' (p.387). Although Darcy's relationship with *her* Kitty is not explicitly stated, and is highly unlikely to be as close, the fact that Kitty's 'improvement was great' (p.385) and that she 'became by proper attention and management, less irritable, less ignorant, and less insipid' (p.385) means that she will be a pleasant and certainly far from scornful addition to their daily lives.

Eventually, the presence of these two young girls means that the Darcys will have to chaperone them to balls and make other efforts to introduce them in their turn to the single men of good fortune of the larger society. However, these social events will be less overwhelming for Darcy than the assembly room ball at the beginning of the novel:

- because he will likely be acquainted with more of those in attendance

- because responsibilities and scripts for his role as host or chaperone will be more clear-cut than are those for an eligible bachelor

- precisely because he will now be in the 'married man' category, fewer will be observing and judging his behaviour; hardly anyone except his lovely Lizzy will be interested in dancing with him anyway!

Their well-being socially will be further enhanced by the marriage of Darcy's closest friend to Elizabeth's closest sister. Both will be able to welcome Mr and Mrs Bingley to their home with alacrity. The frequency of these contacts is guaranteed when the Bingleys 'bought an estate in a neighbouring county to Derbyshire, and Jane and Elizabeth, in addition to every other source of happiness, were within thirty miles of each other' (p.385):

> Austen emphasizes the significance of the close-knit, protective family circle. The unified family circle of sisters...and the two 'brothers,' Darcy and Bingley, close friends who are now brothers-in-law, creates a tightening of family ties. The conclusion is optimistic beyond the satisfactory marriage of the heroine in that it implies that the bonds between the sisters will continue to grow and intensify even after their marriages. (Hudson 1989, p.130)

In terms of further additions to their family circle, among his cousins, Darcy is closest to the gregarious Colonel Fitzwilliam, who already holds positive feelings towards both him and Elizabeth. Since at Rosings the Colonel warned Lizzy that, as a second son, he felt he had to marry with some regard to the fortune of his future life mate, he may himself eventually wed someone with wealth made through trade in her background. Although such a marriage may further 'pollute' Pemberley in his aunt's opinion, the future Mrs Fitzwilliam may provide enriching variety and interest to the social circle of this great estate. She is certainly not likely to look down on its owner or his wife. In both his chosen friends, the Colonel and Bingley, Darcy has models of gentlemen whose easy, polished manners are solidly rooted in a true awareness of and regard for others; over the years, interacting with them can only improve his own.

Most importantly, the family warmly encircling the Darcys includes a happy and long-married couple whom they both respect: 'With the Gardiners, they were always on the most intimate terms. Darcy, as well as Elizabeth, really loved them' (p.388), and were doubtless loved by them in return. Their example and wise counsel also augur well for the future of the Darcys' relationship.

However, in our modern world a marital relationship complicated by ASD would be less likely to draw such a positive although limited social network around it. Given that most people are infinitely more likely to live in crowded urban areas than on great estates, social interactions with many, many more people are required, which can prove stressful for the partner on the spectrum. Since social impairment is one of their core challenges it can lead to isolation if others find the effort of including them continually unrewarding. We can probably all think of couples where we enjoy the one but avoid the other. This may or may not bother the individual with ASD but can be quite depressing for his or her partner, who, due to the marriage, is precisely the person who most needs emotional and social support from the wider world.

Personality traits

Love, freedom from financial worries, close-by and caring friends: truly the Darcys start their married life with many blessings. But still they are who they are. Will Darcy be a good husband? And Elizabeth a good wife?

A 'good' husband? Or a 'good enough' husband? Like most of us, Darcy has many positive traits but also some negative ones. He possesses personal characteristics that will help him be a suitable husband and life companion for Elizabeth in that he is intelligent, loyal, honest, faithful, highly moral and possesses a strong sense of justice. He is also capable of loving and is attracted to people not objects, unlike more severely autistic people; Darcy is not obsessed with the details of Pemberley the way Mr Collins is with Rosings. However, he can be socially awkward and overwhelmed in crowds or among strangers, especially if away from the security of his own home. Particularly when in such settings or at times of high emotion he is less able to participate in conversations, to read the facial and body language of others, or to be aware of the messages his own face and movements are conveying. Therefore, some of his deficits will be most obvious not when he is with Lizzy but rather when he is with others. When Pemberley is the venue for balls for their sisters or later for their children he may become slightly daunted by the number of guests and appear less friendly than expected of a good host. However, these will be rare and temporary situations. Away from these public occasions it is in their most intimate moments, both emotional and sexual, that other of Darcy's challenges due to ASD will be apparent.

Emotionally, as Maxine Aston, herself once married to a man on the spectrum, has written:

> They will give and offer love in the ways that they can... It is unlikely that an AS man will be able to offer emotional support or empathetic feelings. Some women will not be able to live with the emptiness and loneliness that this can bring. (2003, p.197)

Aston conducted numerous in-depth interviews in preparation for writing her book, including approximately 30 with the female partners of men on the autistic spectrum. As quoted previously, she found that:

> All the NT women in the relationships stated that their mental and
> sometimes physical health had suffered as a consequence of being in
> a relationship with an AS man. Many of the NT women were on or
> had been on anti-depressants; they reported feeling exhausted, frus-
> trated, desperate and lonely and many thought they were going
> mad. (2003, p.166)

This level of loneliness and stress is why it is particularly important that anyone in a relationship with an ASD individual also has close access to
supportive friends and family. Fortunate indeed is Lizzy that she and her
husband will be firmly rooted in Pemberley with only their favourites from
among their odd mixture of relatives nearby. In contrast, marrying someone
whose nationality or profession require distant or frequent moves would,
especially in the early months until new contacts are made, put an added
burden on a weak, non-supportive relationship. The modern spouses of that
small proportion of engineers, IT executives or providers of financial services who are on the spectrum face significant challenges essentially alone
when their families are transferred around the country, continent or globe.

From my personal and professional observations the most vulnerable
group of all are those women from impoverished or third world countries
who either met their ASD partner when he was working in their homeland
or whose marriages are of the 'mail order bride' variety. Usually significantly younger than their mate, they tend to have very limited or no control
in the relationship. Their loneliness and isolation can be profound especially
if not fluent in the language of their new country. Often their spouse, due to
his ASD issues, is not well-connected to family members or friends so the
pair are isolated from the community. If and when children result from the
marriage, he may be oblivious to their needs for stimulation or exposure to
the language they will encounter at school. Most of my fellow speech language pathologists will be able to recognize similar sad little family group-
ings on their caseloads; a child with a language delay or autism with a
heart-breakingly lonely, depressed mother and a father who is either
extremely talkative or never available.

However, even with couples who are both from or settled in one place,
deep emotional peaks and valleys occur in life and are best shared. At times
of great joy such as the birth of a child or even just an unexpectedly special
moment, the partner with autism may not be able to match and reflect the
intensity of his or her spouse's emotion. This lack of sharing may lead the
spouse to feel that his or her own positive emotions are dismissed as childish

or excessive, and that life is being pulled down to a grey flatness. Lizzy's liveliness and capacity for joy, whether when dancing or responding to the beauties of nature, may be dampened, if not extinguished, if Darcy is consistently unable to respond in tune with her. Remember that, towards the end of the novel, even when he had just obtained his heart's desire and while his best friend was in the same room joyfully talking and laughing with his fiancée, Darcy sat in silence as he was 'not of a disposition in which happiness overflows in mirth' (p.372).

At the other extreme, at times of sudden injury or loss, the ability of Darcy or those like him to respond appropriately may also be very limited:

> People with AS typically respond best to set schedules, predictable routines, and calm support people. Throw in an unexpected tragedy or two and your partner may tailspin into a meltdown or simply not enter into the situation to help you. There's also the possibility that a person with AS will respond to an emergency situation well, due to his ability to react logically and unemotionally. (Stanford 2003, p.225)

Unfortunately, no one will know which response the individual on the spectrum will make until the emergency is unfolding. One woman told me how her ASD brother-in-law, although very competent in his profession, had 'frozen' or been unable to shift focus when his mother, whom he knew had a history of previous mild strokes, was exhibiting clear signs of having another more major one. Although she apparently approached him and managed a few garbled words, he continued talking on the telephone to a colleague about work. Fortunately, a long-time neighbour, who happened to drop in, recognized the symptoms immediately. Another woman described how her husband, distraught when their pre-schooler was admitted to Accident & Emergency needing to have a lumbar puncture, reacted very angrily towards the medical staff for 'hurting' his beloved child as he was seemingly unable to process the information that this was a necessary, indeed essential, diagnostic procedure.

In cases of death, although they may be extremely helpful and systematic as the executors of a will, they are less likely to serve as comforters of the bereaved. Attwood has commented on how some have a 'tendency to laugh or giggle in circumstances when one would anticipate an expression of…sadness. There have been instances of grief over the death of a member of the family being expressed by laughter…or even indifference' (1998, p.159). If Jane dies in childbirth or one of the Gardiners from illness, how will Darcy care for his wife in her initial anguish? Also, for those on the spectrum, the recovery period from a family death can be extremely quick, with little or no reference ever made to the person again, even in cases of couples who have passed the silver or golden anniversary mark. There can be a stunningly matter-of-fact, 'well, that's over' attitude even following the tragic death of a child or young person.

In addition, it seems particularly hard for a male with ASD to recognize that, to his spouse, a miscarriage is a personal loss to be mourned. Perhaps this partly reflects his difficulties with imagination as the baby was never a visible and concrete part of his life. However, when a wanted pregnancy terminates spontaneously, the mother is usually already deeply in love with the possibility of that child, knows its estimated birth date, and has created dreams and plans around it. Although she is aware that this is not a major loss to the wider world, such a seemingly complete lack of interest from the little one's other parent is unexpected and shattering. If Elizabeth experiences such loss or the death of any of their children her heartbreak may well be increased by the feeling of mourning alone.

If intense emotional intimacy is limited that will also impact on a couple's sexual intimacy. Despite the fact that literally millions of women have pictured themselves in bed with Mr Darcy he will not necessarily be a skilful lover. *They* may have the required imagination but perhaps *he* doesn't! However, just as being handsome doesn't guarantee that he will be passionate, being on the autistic spectrum doesn't guarantee that he won't.

In some sexual relationships no problems occur as for some it will be 'the easiest way to communicate their deepest feelings and show their love for their partner. Sex is a form of communication...[so some AS men] find this way of expressing their feelings far easier than trying to find the right words' (Aston 2003, p.107). If the room is dark or dimly lit the pressure to read their partner's face correctly is removed, as are many of the subtle complex social nuances of life in the full glare of the day. It also may help that in bed there is (usually) just one other person to relate to rather than several!

For other couples sex can be a major disappointment and source of conflict if the 'woodenness' mentioned in social interactions carries over to a similar lack of ease and physicality in the bedroom. With some, their tactile sensitivity makes them avoid even such physical signs of affection as hugs or holding hands let alone extended periods of full body contact. With others their liking for routines and predictability gradually deadens the joy and spontaneity their partner might prefer. The tendency for some with ASD to have weak central coherence may mean that they do not see any connection between the quality of their interactions with their spouse all day and her sexual response to them at night. With others their difficulty with initiating movement or interaction can have a particularly inhibiting effect on the frequency and success of marital relations; so too can their problems correctly interpreting verbal and non-verbal signals.

All these issues probably contributed to the following situation. A woman, who came young and virginal to her wedding bed, told me how her much older husband had lain stiff and unspeaking beside her. When she nervously asked him if they weren't going to 'have a cuddle' he silently rolled over and tried to penetrate her without any sign of affection or foreplay whatsoever. After mere seconds, when the attempt failed, he rolled back to his side of the bed and fell asleep. Apparently when she tried to discuss this abrupt approach to intimacy with him the next day, he was completely oblivious to how deeply upsetting it had been for her. He stated that, having decided not to have sex after the exhausting excitement of the long day of wedding celebrations, he had responded as he did only because she 'had asked'.

'Sexual problems can occur in any relationship whether one of the partners has Asperger syndrome or not. They can be a lot harder to sort out and resolve though with the problems in communication caused by Asperger syndrome' (Aston 2003, p.115). Since Elizabeth's expectations for all aspects of her marital union are set at a higher level than are those of her older friend, Charlotte, there is increased likelihood of dissatisfaction for her:

> *Pride and Prejudice* occupies an intermediate position in [the] history of perspectives on sex and marriage. Austen's novel contains both the older and the newer way of thinking about these matters in the diverging views of Charlotte and Elizabeth. If Charlotte Lucas, with her pragmatic sense that marriage...was preferable to an impoverished and dependent old age, expresses the common wisdom of the seventeenth and early eighteenth centuries, Elizabeth Bennet, with her independent manner...is an example of the newer sort of nineteenth-century heroine...[with her] newer demand for sexual attraction and sentimental love. (Perry 2000, pp.131–32)

As is true for the vast majority of relationships between others, we can speculate on, but never know, what happens after the footmen close the doors to the master bedroom at Pemberley.

Assuming that the sexual side of their marriage is productive, parenting will be the next joy or challenge in Mr and Mrs Darcy's life. Years ago, during a broadcast interview, I heard someone say that, 'The best thing that a man can do for his children is love their mother.' If that foundation is in place then they will be spared the emotional, social and financial traumas of a divorce plus their intact home will probably be a happy, positive, nurturing place. Therefore, Darcy's strong love for their mother is the very bedrock for his children's well-being.

Elizabeth is so unlike her mother that she will not model her maternal style on that she herself experienced. When direct guidance is required she is likely to turn to her Aunt Gardiner, who has the wisdom and experience gleaned from raising four thriving offspring. However, Lizzy's innate energy, intelligence, capacity to love and joyful approach to life will make her a delightful companion for her young children. Her interest in the vagaries of human nature will help her to be sensitive to their individuality. Freed from economic concerns, and from the physical work of feeding and clothing her little ones (no lunch bags or laundry for the mistress of Pemberley), Elizabeth will be able to enjoy her children to the fullest: 'All of Jane Austen's heroines...have the makings of being better mothers than their own; with the self-knowledge they have achieved in the course of the novels, it is quite likely that they will succeed' (Benson 1989, p.124).

Darcy as a father is less predictable. Himself the heir to a great family estate he is almost guaranteed in his turn to expect and desire heirs. Therefore, in principle, the idea of children will be appealing. However, sometimes ASD fathers are particularly prone to jealousy of their own babies when they realize how much of their wife's attention is now elsewhere rather than on them. Again, the Darcys' wealth may cushion them from this challenge as Elizabeth will not need to be constantly caring for and aware of their children the way most working and middle-class young mothers have to be. Lizzy will have the time, flexibility and resources to allow her to be focused on her husband when he wishes.

Unfortunately, a 'father with Asperger syndrome often struggles with adapting to the age of the child and the maturity levels that child is operating at...it is almost impossible for an AS adult to think empathetically on a child's emotional and intellectual level' (Aston 2003, p.97). This may not have been as noticeable in Georgian times as it is now when fathers are expected to take a more active and nurturing role. Fortunately, Mr Darcy, unlike his father-in-law, has already shown that he will ably meet the more traditional roles of provider and protector. It is unlikely that any junior version of Wickham will be able to dally with one of his daughters! Although perhaps not always able to *initiate* exchanges of affection and conversation, if his children are loving and outgoing like their mother, he will often be able to *respond* appropriately to them.

However, what if the random combination of Bennet–Gardiner–Fitzwilliam genes produces one or two Darcy offspring who themselves have some autistic traits? At least two and probably three of their grandparents are on the spectrum, as is their father: 'It has been suggested that when one of the parents has Asperger syndrome there is a one in three chance that a child of that parent will also be on the autistic spectrum' (Aston, 2003, p.220). Tony Attwood, drawing on his years of clinical experience, has observed that:

> [I]f there's been a father with Asperger syndrome with a son with Asperger syndrome, invariably there's been enormous conflict between them. You would hope that [since] they both came from the same planet that they would understand each other but in fact they often push each other away...there can be major fights between them. (2000, p.22)

If neither is easily able to initiate interaction or to appreciate the perspective of the other then there are ample opportunities for conflict. In his family memoir, *A Silver-plated Spoon*, John Russell, the 13th Duke of Bedford, provides striking descriptions of such conflict and lack of connection between four consecutive generations of fathers and sons who were, in the Duke's own words, 'as eccentric as my family is supposed to be'. He records that his father 'broke with his father at the age of twenty-six and I broke with him when I was twenty-two' (1959, p.33). After having been estranged for years, John/Ian (his family even quarrelled over his name so he was registered as one but baptized as the other) records that his father and grandfather did see each other several times shortly before the latter, Herbrand, the 11th Duke, died:

> No attempt was made to rake up old grievances and they spent most of their time talking about the weather or the crops. The atmosphere was clearly at once electric and defensive. I imagine my father was frightened of my grandfather, who could be a very frightening man. They just had these formal conversations because neither of them could talk any other way. I do not think there was ever any paternal

or filial feeling where my father and grandfather were concerned. Neither of them was capable of expressing any emotion, it was quite beyond them. The capacity for expressing affection of any sort was something quite lacking from their temperaments. (p.69)

From my own observations it can sometimes be difficult for the ASD father to realize that his child is not a clone of himself, particularly with a first-born son who often is given a similar name or initials. There can be an automatic assumption that this son will take over the family business or follow the same line of work, even if his talents and interests clearly lie elsewhere (clear to those not afflicted with mindblindness, that is). At times it seems as if the father cannot *imagine* a different sort of life for his son than the one he himself is leading.

Having to try to explain the son to the father and the father to the son will be very taxing for Elizabeth, who will love them both so will find serious conflict between them agonizing. Raising one or more unusually challenging children could affect their marital relationship negatively. Since Paris feels that 'pride' truly is a powerful theme of this novel he feels that it will continue to influence their interactions and satisfaction as a couple:

> Elizabeth and Darcy are bound together by the complex interdependency of their pride systems. The marriage itself fulfills some important needs; it provides recognition and status for Elizabeth, vindication and approval for Darcy... His need to win her approval is matched by her need to think well of him, to share in his grandeur, and to repress her reservations. They are happy at the end because they have a vested interest in exalting each other. This makes for a rewarding, though, I should think, a somewhat tense relationship. They will get along well as long as each continues to feed the other's pride. (Paris 1978, p.139)

The main thing, in my opinion, that could damage that mutual pride is if the heir to Pemberley they produce is noticeably on the autistic spectrum.

So, will Mr and Mrs Darcy live happily ever after or not? The newly engaged Charlotte may have spoken accurately when she referred to the 'chance of happiness' (p.125), as luck or good fortune or chance does play a more major role in anyone's life than we sometimes believe. If the Darcys' children are healthy and neuro-typical, if their family life is relatively uneventful without major disasters such as a fire at Pemberley or a disabling injury…if, if, if…then they will undoubtedly be as happy or happier than most. As cornerstones for their marriage they have the triple blessings of a genuine love for each other, financial security and a small but close circle of positive caring intimates. The shaky fourth stone is the uneasy combination of Elizabeth's high expectations with Darcy's subtle autistic spectrum traits. However, by choosing Elizabeth he has allied himself with the sort of woman who is exactly the type whom Dr Attwood describes as most able to help him: 'somebody who is at the opposite end of the continuum...who is very social, very empathetic, very kind and very caring' (2000, p.19). Darcy told Lizzy that her 'affectionate behaviour to Jane' (p.380) was one of the things that made him love her. Similar kindness to himself will smooth out many difficulties in their years together.

There will be times in their marriage when Elizabeth will be startled and puzzled by the seeming incongruities in her husband's character. However, as a person with a lively, enquiring intelligence always seeking stimulation, that may suit her for, as she herself said: 'intricate characters are the *most* amusing. They have at least that advantage' (p.42).

13

How Did Austen Know?

How did Jane Austen know enough to create characters showing so many subtle characteristics of a syndrome that was not to be medically identified for generations? Just like Leo Kanner and Hans Asperger themselves, she was obviously extremely observant. So, if that answers the 'How?', then the next question is obviously 'Who?' Who were some of the people in her life whose various traits she observed and then incorporated into her fictional creations?

Given that an accurate and official medical diagnosis of an autistic spectrum disorder requires a variety of *behavioural measures*, which usually include a detailed developmental history, various observational checklists and/or theory of mind tasks, it is obviously challenging and unreliable even to speculate about people who have long been lying in the graveyards of southern England. However, Jane's remaining letters in Deidre Le Faye's (1995) definitive compilation do provide a few tantalizing hints about some of her neighbours, both locally and near the home of her brother, Edward Austen Knight, in Kent. Some of these are described below.

Miss Milles

Described in letter #94 as being:

> queer as usual & provided us with plenty to laugh at. She undertook in *three words* to give us the history of Mrs Scudamore's reconciliation, & then talked on about it for half an hour, using such odd expressions & so foolishly minute that I could hardly keep my countenance (p.245).

Mrs Powlett

Referred to in letter #30 as 'saying too little to afford us much amusement' (p.70) while her husband, Revd Charles Powlett, is described by the anonymous author of his obituary as having 'a quick apprehension, and an excellent memory; but he was somewhat deficient in judgement and profundity. His opinions were apt to run to extremes... He was a little too free of his advice, which was given with a self-sufficiency not always well received' (pp.555–6).

Mrs Stephen Terry

About whom, when Jane Austen mentions seeing the newly engaged couple in letter #43, she records that, 'her appearance [is] very quiet. Miss Irvine says she is never speaking a word' (p.99).

Revd Fulwar Craven Fowle

Had been a pupil of George Austen's for three years during Jane's childhood and was a nearby clergyman. According to Deidre Le Faye's biographical index about him in *Jane Austen's Letters*, he is 'remembered by his descendants...as having an impatient and rather irascible nature'. In Letter #32, from Jane to Cassandra, his immaturity and outbursts of temper are mentioned in the context of playing vingt-un, 'which as Fulwar was unsuccessful, gave him an opportunity of exposing himself as usual' (p.75).

Caroline Fowle

Daughter of Revd Fowle, who was then three years of age, is referred to in the same letter as 'very shy, & does not talk much' (p.75).

Others

However, although, as do most of us, Jane Austen had a mix of people among her varied acquaintance, perhaps she did not have to look far from her own family home to gain experience with people who had some characteristics of an autism spectrum disorder.

Her mother's only sister's son, Edward Cooper, a clergyman, is described by one of Austen's biographers as 'less than likeable and in his pomposity and insensitivity seems to have born some resemblance to Mr. Collins.' (Myer 1997, p.140). Certainly, when writing to Cassandra of their sister-in-law's recent death in childbirth, Austen says of Edward Cooper that she hopes 'he will not send one of his Letters of cruel comfort to my poor Brother' (Le Faye, p.148). His son, Edward-Philip Cooper, seems to have been a precocious but unusual child. When Austen hears that he will be attending a boarding school, she notes 'it will be a great change, to become a raw school boy from being a pompous Sermon-Writer, & a domineering Brother.' (p.172)

In her otherwise thriving immediate family there was one brother who was of them but not. The second son, George, who was nearly ten years her senior, is recorded as having suffered from fits or epilepsy. Since he was not developing normally he was never brought back home from his village nurse. Ultimately he ended up living with the same family in Monk Sherborne, Hampshire, who were also caring for his mother's younger brother, Thomas Leigh, who appears to have had similar developmental difficulties. In neither case did these impact on their life expectancy as George lived to the age of 72 while his uncle had surpassed him by attaining 74 years of life.

George's delayed development, long life and his history of seizures are all compatible with a potential diagnosis of autism: 'The prevalence of epilepsy among autistics is much higher then the normal population' and 'children with symptomatic infantile spasms (sudden generalized muscle contractions usually beginning between three and eight months) tend to develop both epilepsy and autism' (Ramanujapuram 2005).

These two close blood relatives show that there might be a familial connection, but they were not part of Jane Austen's day-to-day life nor, with the exception of Miss Anne De Bourgh, does she portray people who are obviously disabled and at the severe end of the spectrum.

Another of her brothers showed possible subtle signs of being at the milder end. The two youngest Austen males of her generation, the sailor brothers and future admirals, may be confused because of their similar careers. However, from the few details we have of them, they emerge as quite different in personality from each other. The younger one, Charles, is described by the well-known Austen scholar Brian Southam as 'blessed with an easy-going nature, and a natural warmth and charm that continued to the very end of his life' (2003, p.38). Southam quotes one of Charles' nephews, who served under him, as writing of him as 'without exception the kindest-hearted and most perfectly gentleman like man I ever knew' (2003, p.39).

These comments differ significantly from Southam's references to the other naval brother, Francis, who is described as 'never popular with his crews', 'a stickler for rules and regulations' and as 'a reserved and private man who kept his deepest feelings to himself' (2003, p.37). He was noted for being 'meticulously detailed' (Lane 1984, p.133) in his reports, while his memoir of his life is rendered distinctively memorable by his '[r]eferring to himself – somewhat disconcertingly – in the third person throughout' (Southam 2003, p.78). Unusual use of pronouns is characteristic of the language problems of some on the spectrum. I have known an adult who often said 'us' when referring to just himself, and have worked with ASD children who have had great difficulty learning the distinction between 'you' and 'I' or between 'he' and 'she'. Donna Williams, a woman with autism, mentions that in school a teacher was mystified when she referred to herself as 'you' in a personal anecdote that she wrote for an assignment.

To add to her possible personal experiences, Jane Austen, like several of her female characters, may have been proposed to by a suitor on the autistic spectrum. While visiting friends at Manydown in December 1802, she received and accepted an offer of marriage from their younger brother but then abruptly withdrew from the commitment the next morning. Harris Bigg-Wither was, according to one biographer, a 'rather shy and shambling young man of twenty-one with a serious stutter and an oddly blunted intelligence' (Shields 2001, p.106), while another refers to him as a 'shy, stammering boy' who had matured into a man 'still awkward in manner' (Tomalin 1997, p.182). He had been privately educated at home for longer than usual, ostensibly because of his communication problems, which are also put forward as reasons why 'social life could be something of an ordeal, and made him occasionally aggressive' (p.182). These few descriptors certainly could indicate a man who might be on the autistic spectrum. Professionally, I have worked with three boys who showed significant problems with fluency in addition to being diagnosed as ASD. Given that both issues can be accompanied by problems with oral–motor planning, they are certainly not incompatible conditions.

As I mentioned earlier, in *Pride and Prejudice* Jane Austen's characters with ASD portray a sex ratio that is markedly different from reality. Particularly the mild or Asperger's range is so heavily a male condition that Professor Simon Baron-Cohen even gives presentations entitled 'Is Autism an Extreme Form of Maleness?' Given how many other characteristics Jane Austen 'got right', what could explain why she got this blatantly noticeable characteristic 'wrong'? One likely reason is that her own personal experience may have happened to include an unusually high number of women.

One rather distinctive and prominent female relative in her life was her mother's only brother's wife, Jane Cholmeley Leigh-Perrot. One biographer notes that, in her letters, Jane Austen 'never missed an opportunity to call attention to the absurdity of Mrs Leigh Perrot's thoughts and actions' (Tucker 1983, p.92). He describes her as 'a formidable and opinionated woman' who 'dearly loved a bargain' (p.82), and notes that in one of her own letters she describes herself by writing, 'I cannot dissemble with anyone...if I am angry all must know it – if I am miserable I cannot hide it' (p.82). Some of these characteristics are shared by the fictional Lady Catherine, while an excessive frugality or delight in saving a few pennies even when wealthy has been commented on as a trait of some with ASD.

But again, perhaps we do not need to look away from Jane Austen's intimate circle even so far as to an aunt by marriage. Given that Jane spent her life living with her, there are remarkably few references to her mother, Cassandra Leigh Austen, in her letters. I should say in her *surviving* letters. Jane's sister, Cassandra, according to their niece, Caroline, treasured all of the author's letters until near the end of her long life, when she 'looked them over and burnt the greater part' (Tomalin 1997, p.284). When her parents decided, without consulting their adult but dependent daughters, to move their foursome from their Steventon home of over 30 years to Bath, family lore has it that Jane Austen fainted due to the sudden and disagreeable shock: 'Cassandra destroyed several letters Jane wrote to her immediately after hearing her parents' decision, which suggest they made her uncomfortable, too full of raw feeling and even anger' (1997, p.171).

So much scholarship surrounding Jane Austen herself and the circumstances that shaped her novels involves speculating about tiny scraps of information left behind by people who would have been incredulous had they known that they are of interest to strangers centuries later due to their relationship to one of the seemingly least important members of their family, an almost penniless younger daughter and maiden aunt. Our impressions are only precisely that, faint impressions, so they may be as unreliable as the first impressions that Elizabeth formed of Darcy and Wickham. However, several recent biographers have commented uneasily on Jane's relationship to her mother. Claire Tomalin writes that '[i]n Jane's case, the emotional distance between child and mother is obvious throughout her life' (1997, p.6), while Carol Shields, the devoted mother of four daughters herself, observes that 'a close bond between mothers and daughters is rare in the Austen novels' (2001, p.16). She adds that:

> Of Jane Austen's mother we know only a little... Suggested glimpses of hypochondria or peevishness envelop her in later life – each of these glimpses gestures toward and secures a hundred

others, as is often the case when biographical documentation is scarce. Jane Austen, in her final illness, reports she was too weak to walk upstairs and so she sometimes rested on three sitting-room chairs lined up together, leaving the sofa for her mother. What can we make of this improbable scene? Did her mother not notice the unusual furniture deployment? Or was Jane Austen in the full throes of a bizarre martyrdom? Were the mother and daughter playing out an old and rivalrous claim? Or was Mrs Austen – and this is the interpretation that has hardened in the record – a *demanding and self-absorbed* woman, careless of her daughter's comfort and *too insensitive* to see the signs of serious illness? (2001, p.17, my italics)

We can speculate and sift through the already harvested chaff for any previously overlooked grains of information, but we cannot be sure. Given that individuals on the autistic spectrum are puzzling enough to understand even when they live and breathe among us, those in the dust of time are impossible for us to decipher.

Some chat lines even include Jane herself among their lists of famous and creative people who may have shown some autistic traits. Obviously, the research needed to defend or debunk such comments is significantly beyond the scope of this book. However, given the strong indications of a history of ASD in her family, it is possible that Jane may have had mild traces of one or two traits that would place her in the group sometimes referred to, colloquially or on the Internet, as 'autistic cousins'.

Whoever her sources were, we are fortunate that, in Jane Austen's mere 41 years of life, she appears to have met, observed and been intrigued by a sufficient number of people on the autistic spectrum to incorporate many of their traits into her unforgettable characters in *Pride and Prejudice*. They have captured the hearts and fascinated the minds of millions ever since.

In the day-to-day reality of our non-fiction world, the majority of us have met one or two similarly intricate and unique individuals. It is my hope, in some cases, that our new knowledge about the autistic spectrum has partially solved the puzzle of their personalities so we can share our lives with them with less bewilderment and more understanding.

References

Arthur, S. (2005) *Dating Mr Darcy: The Smart Girl's Guide To Sensible Romance*. Wheaten, IL: Tyndale House Publishers Inc.

Aston, M. (2001) *The Other Half of Asperger Syndrome*. London: National Autistic Society.

Aston, M. (2003) *Aspergers in Love: Couple Relationships and Family Affairs*. London: Jessica Kingsley Publishers.

Attwood, T. (1998) *Asperger's Syndrome: A Guide for Parents and Professionals*. London: Jessica Kingsley Publishers.

Attwood, T. (2000) *Workshop for Partners of People with Asperger's Syndrome*. London: The National Autistic Society. www.nas.org.uk/content/1/c4/36/attwood2.pdf

Attwood, T. (2002) *The Profile of Friendship Skills in Asperger's Syndrome*. www.tonyattwood.com.au

Attwood, T. (2007) *The Complete Guide to Asperger's Syndrome*. London: Jessica Kingsley Publishers.

Austen, J. (1986) *Northanger Abbey*. Ed. R.W. Chapman, third edn. Oxford: OUP. (First edition 1933.)

Austen, J. (1988) *Pride and Prejudice*. Ed. R.W. Chapman, third edn. Oxford: OUP. (First edition 1933.)

Barnhill, G.P. (2002) *Right Address...Wrong Planet: Children with Asperger Syndrome Becoming Adults*. Shawnee Mission, KS: Autism Asperger Publishing Company.

Baron, M.G., Grooden, J., Grooden, G. and Lipsitt, L.P. (eds) (2006) *Stress and Coping in Autism*. Oxford: Oxford University Press.

Baron-Cohen, S. (2006) *Is Autism an Extreme Form of the Male Brain? The Fetal Androgen Theory of Autism*. Presentation given at the Wosk Centre for Dialogue, Simon Fraser University, 6 October.

Bayley, J. (1968) 'The "irresponsibility" of Jane Austen.' In B.C. Southam (ed.) *Critical Essays on Jane Austen*. London: Routledge & Kegan Paul Ltd.

Benson, M.M. (1989) 'Mothers, substitute mothers, and daughters in the novels of Jane Austen.' *Persuasions: The Jane Austen Journal 11*, 117–124.

Brown, J. (2003) 'Miniatures: Mary Bennet: A young lady of deep reflection.' *Jane Austen's Regency World 5*, 38–39.

Donnellan, A.M. and Robledo, J.A. (2006) *Autism, Stress, and Movement Differences: Supporting Individuals Through Relationships*. Proceedings of the ASA 37th National Conference, 12–15 July 2006, 94.

Ellio, M. (2005) 'Trade.' In J. Todd (ed.) *Jane Austen in Context*. Cambridge: University Press.

Emsley, S. (2005) *Jane Austen's Philosophy of the Virtues*. New York: Palgrave Macmillan.

Emsley, S. (2006) 'Laughing at our neighbours: Jane Austen and the problem of charity.' *Persuasions: The Jane Austen Journal Online 26*, 1.

Foster Stovel, N. (2002) 'Famous last words: Elizabeth Bennet protests too much.' In B. Stovel and L. Weinlos Gregg (eds) *The Talk in Jane Austen*. Edmonton: University of Alberta Press.

Frith, U. and Happe, F. (1999) 'Theory of mind and self-consciousness: What is it like to be autistic?' *Mind and Language 14*, 1, 1–22.

Garcia Winner, M. (2002) *Thinking About YOU Thinking about ME*. London: Jessica Kingsley Publishers.

Gilberg, C. (1998) 'Asperger Syndrome and High-Functioning Autism.' *British Journal of Psychiatry 171*, 200–209.

Gilman, P. (2000) 'Disarming proof': *Pride and Prejudice* and the power of criticism.' *Persuasions: The Jane Austen Journal 22*, 218–229.

Glancy, K. (1989) 'What happened next? or The many husbands of Georgiana Darcy.' *Persuasions: The Jane Austen Journal 11*, 110–116.

Grandin, T. (1992) 'An inside view of autism.' In E. Schopler and G.B. Mesibov (eds) *High Functioning Individuals with Autism*. New York: Plenum Press.

Grandin, T. (1995) *Thinking in Pictures*. New York: Doubleday.

Grandin, T. and Scariano, M.M. (1986) *Emergence: Labeled Autistic*. New York: Warner Books.

Grice, H.P. (1975) 'Logic and conversation.' In R. Cole and J. Morgan (eds) *Syntax and Semantics: Speech Acts*. New York: Academic Press.

Grinker, R.R. (2007) *Unstrange Minds: Remapping the World of Autism*. Cambridge, MA: Basic Books.

Gutstein, S. (2000) *Autism/Asperger's: Solving the Relationship Puzzle*. Arlington, TX: Future Horizons.

Haddon, M. (2002) *The Curious Incident of the Dog in the Night-time*. Toronto: Doubleday Canada.

Hadjikhani, N., Joseph, R.M., Synder, J., Chabris, C.F. *et al.* (2004) 'Activation of the fusiform gyrus when individuals with autism spectrum disorder view faces.' *NeuroImage 22*, 1141–1150.

Halperin, J. (1989) 'Inside *Pride and Prejudice*.' *Persuasions: The Jane Austen Journal 11*, 37–46.

Harding, D.W. (1968) 'Character and caricature in Jane Austen.' In B.C. Southam (ed.) *Critical Essays on Jane Austen*. London: Routledge & Kegan Paul Ltd.

Herrle, J. (2002) 'The idiolects of the idiots: The language and conversation of Jane Austen's less-than-savoury suitors.' In B. Stovel and L. Weinlos Gregg (eds) *The Talk in Jane Austen*. Edmonton: University of Alberta Press.

Holliday Willey, L. (1999) *Pretending to be Normal: Living with Asperger's Syndrome*. London: Jessica Kingsley Publishers.

Hudson, G.A. (1989) 'Sibling love in Jane Austen's *Pride and Prejudice*.' *Persuasions: The Jane Austen Journal 11*, 125–131.

Jennings Linehan, S. (2004) 'Parenting problems for parents with Asperger's Syndrome: A commentary for Aspar rather than AS as parenting disability'. Accessed on 9 August 2006 at www.aspires-relationships.com/articles_commentary_for_aspires.htm.

Joliffe, T., Lansdown, R. and Robinson, C. (1992) 'Autism: A personal account.' *Communication, Journal of the National Autistic Society 26*, 12–19.

Jones, C. (2005) 'Landownership.' In Todd, J. (ed.) *Jane Austen in Context*. Cambridge: Cambridge University Press.

Keymer, T. (2005) 'Rank.' In Todd, J. (ed.) *Jane Austen in Context*. Cambridge: Cambridge University Press.

Laidler, J.R. (2004) *The 'Refrigerator Mother' Hypothesis of Autism*. www.autism-watch.org/causes/rm.shtml

Lane, M. (1984) *Jane Austen's Family: Through Five Generations*. London: Robert Hale Ltd.

Laskin, D. and Hughes, H. (1995) *The Reading Group Book*. New York: Penguin Books.

Laughlin Adler, B. (2002) '"A disagreement between us": Gendered argument in Austen's novels.' *Persuasions: The Jane Austen Journal 24*, 164–176.

Le Faye, D. (ed.) (1995) *Jane Austen's Letters*. Oxford: Oxford University Press.

Lynn, G.T. (1999) 'Five survival strategies to help children with Asperger's syndrome overcome inertia.' Accessed on 17 March 2007 at www.childspirit.com/onlinearts.htm.

Mann, B.A. (2002) '"Your portion is unhappily so small": Jane Austen and the dreadful proposal.' *Persuasions: The Jane Austen Journal 24*, 201–207.

McMaster, J. (2001) 'Reading body language: A game of skill.' *Persuasions: The Jane Austen Journal 23*, 90–104.

Moon, E. (2002) *The Speed of Dark.* London: Orbit UK.

Myer, V.G. (1997) Jane Austen: Obstinate Heart. New York: Arcade Publishing.

National Institute of Health (2007) *Autism Research at the NICHD.* Accessed on 5 November 2006 at www.nichd.nih.gov/autism

Nazeer, K. (2006) *Send in the Idiots: Or How We Grew to Understand the World.* London: Bloomsbury Publishing plc.

Niemark, J. (2007) 'Autism: It's Not Just in the Head.' *Discover*, April 2007, 33–38.

Paris, B.J. (1978) *Character and Conflict in Jane Austen's Novels: A Psychological Approach.* Detroit, MI: Wayne State University Press.

Perry, R. (2000) 'Sleeping with Mr Collins.' *Persuasions: The Jane Austen Journal 22*, 131–132.

Ramanujapuram, A. (2005) 'Autism and epilepsy: The complex relationship between cognition, behaviour and seizures.' *Internet Journal of Neurology 4*, 1.

Ratey, J.J. and Johnson, C. (1997) *Shadow Syndromes: The Mild Forms of Major Mental Disorders that Sabotage Us.* New York: Bantam Books.

Rubin, K. and Thompson, A. (2002) *The Friendship Factor: Helping Our Children Navigate their Social World – and Why it Matters for their Success and Happiness.* New York: Viking.

Russell, J. (1959) *A Silver-plated Spoon.* London: Cassell and Company Ltd.

Scott, S.D. (2002) 'Making room in the middle: Mary in *Pride and Prejudice*.' In B. Stovel and L. Weinlos Gregg (eds) *The Talk in Jane Austen.* Edmonton: University of Alberta Press.

Sherrod, B. (1989) '*Pride and Prejudice*: a classic love story.' *Persuasions: The Jane Austen Journal*, 11, 66–69.

Shields, C. (2001) *Jane Austen.* Harmondsworth, Middlesex: Penguin Books Ltd.

Southam, B. (2003) 'Jane Austen's sailor brothers: Francis and Charles in life and in art.' *Persuasions: The Jane Austen Journal 25*, 33–45.

Southam, B. (2005) 'Professions.' In J. Todd, (ed.) *Jane Austen in Context.* Cambridge: Cambridge University Press.

Stanford, A. (2003) *Asperger Syndrome and Long-term Relationships.* London: Jessica Kingsley Publishers.

Thompson, A. (1999) 'The felicities of rapid motion: Jane Austen in the ballroom.' *Persuasions Online 21*, 1, 1–6.

Tomalin, C. (1997) *Jane Austen: A Life.* London: Penguin Books Ltd.

Tucker, G.H. (1983) *A Goodly Heritage: A History of Jane Austen's Family.* Manchester: Carcanet New Press.

Twachtman-Cullen, D. (2006) 'Communication and stress in students with autism spectrum disorders.' In M.G. Baron, J. Groden, G. Groden and L.P. Lipsitt (eds) *Stress and Coping in Autism.* Oxford: University Press.

Vickery, A. (1998) *The Gentleman's Daughter: Women's Lives in Georgian England.* New Haven, CT: Yale University Press.

Wing, L. (1981) 'Asperger's Syndrome: a clinical account.' *Psychological Medicine 11*, 115–130.

Wing, L. (1992) 'Manifestations of social problems in high functioning autistic people.' In E. Schopler and G. Mesibov (eds) *High Functioning Individuals with Autism.* New York: Plenum Press.

Wing, L. and Shah, A. (2000) 'Catatonia in autistic spectrum disorders.' *British Journal of Psychiatry 176*, 357–362.

Index